The Millionaire Within

Walter Wisniewski
Allison Vanaski

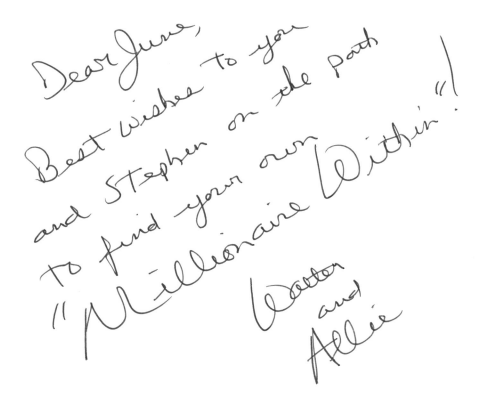

Dear June,
Best wishes to you
and Stephen on the path
to find your own
"Millionaire Within"!

Walter
and
Allie

The Millionaire Within
Copyright ©2017 Walter Wisniewski and Allison Vanaski

ISBN 978-1506-905-11-2 HC
ISBN 978-1506-905-12-9 PBK
ISBN 978-1506-905-13-6 EBK

LCCN 2017958429

December 2017

Published and Distributed by
First Edition Design Publishing, Inc.
P.O. Box 20217, Sarasota, FL 34276-3217
www.firsteditiondesignpublishing.com

This publication is designed to provide accurate and authoritative information in regard to the subject matter covered. It is sold with the understanding that neither the Author nor the Publisher is held responsible for the reader's actions. All investments hold risks that the reader should understand those risks thoroughly.

We would like to dedicate this book to all those who are willing to explore a new approach to life and money and become empowered to discover their own Millionaire Within!

Acknowledgements

*"At times, our own light goes out and is
rekindled by a spark from another person. Each
of us has cause to think with deep gratitude of
those who have lighted the flame within us."*
Albert Schweitzer

There were many influential people involved in the creation of our book. We are grateful to each and every one of them for their assistance, especially...

Our friends and family who supported us with their patience, consideration and encouragement over the years. They were major motivating factors in the development of our story.

Our clients who openly discussed the challenges they face every day which were the basis for the solutions we have offered to our readers.

Our patient and flexible staff at Arcadia, especially Sara Stollberger, who have allowed us to take the time out of our busy day to write our book.

The late Dr. Wayne Dyer, whose wisdom and knowledge has been a great inspiration in my life.

The writings of Anthony de Mello and others like him, whose commitment to serving others has changed the course of human history.

The community of our financial planning peers who have served as a source of wisdom that has enriched the knowledge of our profession and allowed us to share their ideas in our book. In particular I would like to thank Andy Rich, John Trotta, Rich Bergen, Bob Kleinman, Tony Papa, Dan Mazzola, Alex Wasilewski and Michael Goodman.

Weston Wellington from Dimensional Fund Advisors for his intuitive discussions on people, business and the academic research imbedded in his investment philosophy.

Dimensional Fund Advisors for their incredible academic research and the resources they provide. We would like to especially thank the advisors in our Study Group who always have such wonderful ideas on how to better serve our clients. We would also like to thank Hunt Cairns, Stephen Kurad, and Apollo Lupescu for their ideas and support over the years.

Marc Klee whose valuable friendship and advice shaped our careers and provided insight and guidance in the development of our book.

Dr. Charlotte Tomaino whose conversation with us expanded our knowledge on the intricacies of the brain and how it affects our emotions and behavior.

Our coaches, consultants and therapists, especially Laurie Gripshover Taylor, Ginny Hudgens, and Larry Zuckerman, for keeping us sane.

My wonderful friend, Rich Snee, Columbia University graduate and fellow cross-country teammate on our ninth grade high school track team, who assisted in editing our book. Thanks for all your time and energy!

My dear friend Renée Kappen whose memories of my family helped shape into words the deeply moving and emotional story that became the inspiration for my career in financial planning. Her patience and expert editing were very much appreciated.

Michael Dubes whose creative insight and editorial expertise was everything a writer could ask for in an editor.

For anyone we overlooked, we thank you for your support and encouragement throughout this journey.

Table of Contents

Preface

"There's no scarcity of opportunity to make a living at what you love. There is only a scarcity of resolve to make it happen."
Wayne Dyer

My daughter Allie and I decided to write this book together because we wanted to share our mutual experiences in helping our clients and other investors change their perceptions about money. Most people consult financial publications hoping to gain insights into "new" financial strategies or to find promising investments for the upcoming year. In essence, they erroneously seek answers by attempting to choose the best stocks, timing the markets, or discovering the next hot sector.

If anyone — a financial advisor, stock analyst, economist or crystal ball gazer — actually had a method of accurately predicting what the markets were going to do next week or next year, why would they spend their time writing a book or advising others? Why wouldn't they simply apply that knowledge and become a millionaire themselves?

However, Allie and I know that people tend to succeed or fail with their finances based on their perceptions, behaviors and biases about money, not because they choose the right stocks at the right time! The sooner investors have this epiphany, the sooner they will make better informed financial decisions. A marvelous byproduct of this "Aha" moment is that they will come to enjoy what they already have and worry less about what they don't have. It is quite a transformational experience which Allie and I have seen occur countless times with our clients.

Walter's Experience

As a teenager I absorbed a great deal about life and money just by watching and listening to my parents. My father toiled as an airplane mechanic in the 1950s, working alongside hazardous materials, making very little money in order to provide for his family. Receiving a nickel-an-hour raise was cause for celebration in our home!

My mother had an equally difficult and frustrating life, laboring as a seamstress in a sewing factory sweatshop until eleven o'clock each night. After years of struggle and saving, they accumulated enough money to buy a small general store in our blue collar neighborhood on Long Island. My father borrowed money from friends and relatives for the meager down payment to finance this business venture.

Both my parents worked from seven in the morning until eleven each night...the first self-proclaimed 7-11 in America! In my early teens, while working daily in the store, I acquired a sound work ethic, accompanied by traits that would serve me well later in life. Working in the delicatessen and engaging with hard-working families taught me so much about the value people placed on the money they spent and what they expected in return.

Our family operated store was based on trust; no one took a salary. If we needed money, we took what was absolutely necessary from the cash register. Money was constantly an issue that concerned my parents, because there never seemed to be enough. However, even amid their financial insecurity my parents exhibited enormous generosity toward our neighborhood customers, many of whom were suffering financial hardships. My parents frequently extended credit to them, which most of the time was never repaid. These sincere acts of kindness caused additional stress to our family.

Unfortunately, because of this, the business never generated enough money to support us. My mother had to take a second job to make ends meet. The stress and financial pressure of the failing store eventually forced my parents to borrow money against the little equity they had in our house. The situation began to unravel because they were siphoning money from our home to keep the business afloat. Fear of failure and deep emotional connection to the store and their customers caused them to continue to work in a business that was slowly eating away the only savings they had.

In the late 1960s, disaster struck. My twenty year-old brother, who was a senior in college, was killed instantly when his Volkswagen Beetle was struck by a drunk driver head on. I was fourteen at the time and it was a pivotal and defining moment for our family...a nightmare from which we would never awake.

My parents lost interest in their store as quickly as they lost themselves in alcohol. Eventually the business failed and the store was forever shuttered. I witnessed firsthand how my parents squandered what little money remained until it disappeared completely because life lost all meaning for them. The emotional anguish which accompanied the death of their oldest son totally obliterated the future for them and caused them to make poor decisions with their money. Interestingly enough, the coping skills and life lessons I learned to survive this period in my life have remained useful to me over the years.

The major reason I went into financial services is that I never wanted my children to struggle in the same way as my parents. I never wanted money to be an issue for my family. As my career progressed, I found myself working to achieve the same goals for my clients as I did for my own family. I enjoyed helping others find security after experiencing *insecurity* in my own life.

I became aware of the connection between people's emotions and behaviors and how it affected their perception of money. Later in life, when I was able to help my parents with their finances, my father would break down in tears when I was generous with him and my mother. As a son providing for his parents, I learned firsthand how important it was for my clients to achieve financial freedom. I realized I had the power to make a major difference in the lives of many people.

During my early years as a wealth manager, I was more successful than my parents had been in their lifetime. However, when the market crashed in 1987, I allowed my emotions to obstruct my judgment and I made poor investments in the real estate and stock markets. It not only bothered me that I lost a considerable amount of money but also that I lost the connection with my family, just as my father had done years before.

The 1987 market crash and the ensuing real estate losses were a serious setback for me. I knew I had to make a change and realized that could only come about if I changed the way I thought about things. A few years later, I noticed there was a platform for fee-only financial advisors at one of the big brokerage firms. I decided to start my own company and a few former clients offered to move with me to my new firm. It was a big risk but one I knew I had to take if I was to find peace and contentment. It was during this period that I learned an important lesson: *every failure contains the seeds for future success.*

What had been a catastrophic financial loss became an opportunity to move in a different direction. As a result, I found greater success and a sense of self-fulfillment. The reason I am writing this book is because I have discovered the millionaire in me, and want to share it with others.

Allie's Experience

Every family has unique circumstances which shape their lives. For me, our family tragedy was peppered throughout my life, as I am not sure a parent could ever recover from the loss of a son, nor a sibling ever recover from the loss of an older brother. Our extended family grew very close over the years and I can't recall a weekend going by without spending time with my grandparents, pitching pennies or making up silly rhymes.

For as long as I can remember, my family had a strong bond. It was clear my Papa would do anything for those he cared about, traits passed along to my dad as he raised me and my siblings. Because of this, I had the benefit of growing up in an environment of stability and support. Generations of owning small family businesses taught me the value of a dollar at an early age, either through earning a weekly allowance or making change in the liquor store my grandparents owned later in life.

My father was a hard-worker, always providing for his family, even when money may have been tight. One year as Christmas approached, I overheard a conversation between my parents. My mom was telling my dad there was only $99 left in the bank and she wasn't sure how they were going to pay for the upcoming bills. Christmas came and went with plenty of presents to open and the worried tones of my parents were soon forgotten. As a parent myself, I understand how real those conversations and concerns about money can be, forgotten when seeing how happy your children are.

For the most part, I grew up attuned to my dad's quality relationships with his clients, overhearing how he was able to help others with their finances, and the impact he had on their personal lives. His clients were always a big part of our family—I remember them attending my birthday or graduation parties, many of whom are still clients today.

When I was 14 my Papa died from a heart attack. The wake and funeral celebrating his life were packed, a testament to how many lives he had touched in his 75 years. Many of the funeral directors were surprised at the crowds, commenting on how Papa's funeral looked more like a child's funeral than that of an old man. But it wasn't surprising to me, or to my dad. My Papa was loved by everyone he met; his conversations and jokes were a legacy not to be forgotten. It's ironic to think he died of a heart attack, a man's heart so strong: survived by the death of a child, the failure of a business, propped up by the strength of his family, and the many friends he made over the years. It's interesting that even though I was only 14, I knew Papa did not have a lot of money, but he loved and he cared about others. In the end, that's all that really matters. Knowing my father's story and what his family went through, I discovered how emotions can become so powerful it's impossible to think clearly. But I also know that people will persevere.

Years later I graduated Villanova University where I majored in Finance. My first job was with Lehman Brothers in the Compliance department. I wasn't sure if my entry-level position was my dream job, but my proverbial foot was in the door and I dove headfirst into the corporate world with my new wardrobe of suits.

Seven years into my career on Wall Street, I felt as though something was missing. I longed for the personal relationships my father had formed in his financial planning business. Too often I felt as though I was just another face in a cubicle, not making much of an impact on people's lives.

One night after work I received a phone call from my dad. He mentioned his business was growing and he needed to hire someone.

"What about me?" I asked. "You know I always wanted to work with you. It was just a matter of when I thought I was ready. I'm ready."

Surprisingly, my dad had no idea I entertained that desire. Evidently, while I was off trying to gain some experience on my own, he assumed I had no interest in my joining him in his practice. We hit the ground running, working closely together to transition the business to better serve our clients.

When I reflect on how my dad's practice has evolved over the years, and how I felt it prudent to join in on his venture, I know my grandfather would have been so proud. My father and I know the importance of family. Family is the reason my dad started his business. Family is the reason I *joined* the business. And if together, we can help families feel secure about their finances, find happiness and fulfillment on their path, then we as a family, and as our clients' advisors, have truly succeeded. By joining my dad in writing this book, we will share our journey to help you and others find their *millionaire within.*

The Millionaire Within

Walter Wisniewski
Allison Vanaski

Introduction

Money affects every aspect of our lives. It influences our financial circumstances, of course, but also our relationships with friends, business associates and our family. It even affects the way we define our values and sense of self-worth.

My daughter Allie and I wrote this book to help you conquer the fears, biases and emotions that inhibit you from feeling confident about the future. You will learn fundamental techniques that we've taught others to overcome the stress and anxiety associated with managing their money. This straightforward approach can work equally well for you. The wisdom you have gained from your financial mistakes in the past can become the foundation for a more resilient financial future. You will come to understand that whatever adversity you have suffered, you are not alone and the obstacles can be overcome.

After forty years of helping clients plan for their financial futures, I've seen innumerable examples of men and women whose emotional challenges and early childhood experiences with money have led them to believe they are undeserving of wealth or abundance later in life. This unease with prosperity is not confined to people from a specific environment or social class. I've known highly successful executives and entrepreneurs who confidently make critical business decisions but become immobilized when faced with personal financial choices.

The smartest people often make the biggest mistakes with their money, errors they might easily have avoided had their emotions and biases not interfered with their judgment. People of all levels of intelligence, education and accomplishment regularly let their predispositions and learned behaviors get in the way of reaching their financial goals. Just as important, by overcoming these tendencies, we can create a sense of inner peace and the potential for a purposeful, fulfilling life.

We teach our clients that becoming a millionaire depends neither on the return they get from their investments, nor even on the amount of wealth they accumulate. Finding the millionaire within is discovering the riches money can't buy. This includes good health, a fulfilling job or career, and the tranquility of achieving control over our emotions and fears about money.

When we meet with prospective clients, our initial conversations are typically not about investment strategies or returns. We talk instead about what money means to them. They share their thoughts and concerns, often expressing a desire to achieve or maintain a certain lifestyle without the fear of losing or outliving their money. Many worry about someday becoming dependent upon their children. Their fears are often based on youthful experiences regarding how their parents handled money. They may not even be aware that they have acquired financial biases based on those experiences.

Everyone has a different perspective when it comes to money. What does money mean to you? Maintaining your lifestyle? A fulfilling retirement? Leaving a legacy?

What worries you regarding money? What are your worst financial fears?

When you find the millionaire within, you will begin changing your perceptions and discarding your illogical biases about money. While this book will certainly help you become a better investor, we are not going to talk to you about timing the market or finding the next hot stock. This is not a book about financial planning or how to invest. There are plenty of those gathering dust on bookstore shelves. This is an investment book but it's not about investment mechanics. It's about your perceptions and your capacity to change.

Remember this: *intelligent financial decision making has little or nothing to do with money. It has to do with your emotions and behavior.* At some point, emotions and biases cloud everyone's judgment. It's human nature. But investing is not about money; it's about your life.

A man whose writing we greatly admire is the late Wayne Dyer. One of his beliefs is that if you have a problem with someone, the solution isn't about getting that person to change; the solution is within you. You have to change, and when you do, the people around you will change too. To quote Wayne, *"Change the way you look at things and the things you look at change."*

We believe it's the same with money. When your ideas about money change, the concept of money changes. Because your perception has changed, your interaction with money changes. In the process, you come to understand yourself better.

This better understanding brings with it a sense of peacefulness. You experience *a paradigm shift* in how you see things.

A true story by Frank Koch that first appeared in *Proceedings*, the magazine of the Naval Institute, illustrates the point. A battleship was conducting exercises in foggy weather. Just after dark, the lookout spotted a light on the starboard side. The captain asked if it was steady or moving.

"Steady" replied the lookout, which meant they were on direct collision course with the ship!

The captain ordered the lookout to signal the other ship: "Change course 20 degrees; we are on a collision course with you."

The response: "Advisable for you to change course."

The angry captain signaled back: "I am a captain. Change your course 20 degrees."

Response: "I am a seaman second class and you had better change your course 20 degrees."

Now furious, the captain retorted: "I am a battleship. Change course!"

Back came the signal: "I am a lighthouse."

The captain changed course.

It was a great lesson for the captain, who learned to see things differently. Had he not, the lives of the ship's crew would have been jeopardized. In much the same way, our loved ones rely on us to make informed money decisions. To do so, we must be able to see things clearly.

This book will help you make better financial decisions. It will help you find the *millionaire within* so you can achieve a secure, tranquil financial future.

Chapter One

Knowing Yourself and Your Behaviors

"When a man is prey to his emotions,
he is not his own master."
Baruch Spinoza

Ask a hundred people whether their emotions influence their financial decisions and all but a few will say "no." Most people believe they approach investing and money matters with a sound, analytical state of mind. In reality, they approach investing from an emotional perspective.

The result of your relationship with money should be to find happiness and fulfillment. Success is not measured by getting rich quick or outperforming the market. Finding your *Millionaire Within* is a process that helps you discover both financial security and personal fulfillment so you can achieve the life you want to live.

Most people are unaware that their emotions and biases are having an influence on how they view money and investing. Their only clue comes from their past financial mistakes and even then, many people refuse to acknowledge their blunders.

Fear, greed and other emotions cause people to act impulsively. Frightened investors lose their ability to think clearly. When markets go down, they panic and abandon their investment plan — if they have one — and liquidate their assets at depressed prices. They feel temporarily relieved but soon discover a new anxiety: missing out on the market recovery. Investors who flee the market because of a downturn forget that they ultimately have to decide when to reinvest!

Events outside of the financial markets can also trigger inappropriate responses, for example, a previous traumatic experience can make it difficult to make sound financial decisions.

One of our clients, a baby boomer, inherited a large amount of money at an early age. She has a portfolio worth over two million dollars but for the past ten years has kept roughly half of it in a bank savings account, earning a paltry return that doesn't even keep up with inflation. She is afraid of investing for fear she will make a mistake and lose her money.

We continuously ask her about her interests and what she wants to do with her life and her money, but each time we broach the subject, she responds by asking us about world events so she can decide where best to invest her money. She constantly watches the financial news shows and tries to connect the impact of their conversations with her portfolio. In our attempts to educate her, we discovered there are important behavioral issues that make her afraid to invest her money. But she is paralyzed by this fear. Despite our efforts and assurances, she continues down the same path, leaving much of her money in the bank, its purchasing power eroding every year. While she seems to understand and agree with what we suggest, her past experiences have left her confused and immobilized and she is simply unable to change.

The first step in overcoming harmful behaviors is to admit you've made mistakes in the past. Once you identify this pattern — the quirks, idiosyncrasies, biases and behaviors that caused your financial missteps — you can begin making the adjustments that will help you avoid repeating those mistakes.

> *"How you react emotionally*
> *is a choice in any situation."*
> Judith Orloff

Opportunities for Success

You don't need a financial planning textbook to help you overcome bad money behaviors or relearn the proper way to invest money. You don't have to spend endless hours studying stock charts, trying to build the optimal portfolio. You don't have to stay glued to 24/7 financial news reports. The answers may be right in front of you, or more accurately, right inside you. Most important, just because you failed in the past is no reason you can't reach financial security. Adversity can be an opportunity to build success if you understand the behaviors that are causing you to make mistakes.

Investing involves the unknown. It's not possible to know the future. There is an almost limitless number of factors that influence the direction of the markets. It's impossible for anyone, no matter how knowledgeable or diligent, to assimilate all these elements into a strategy that accurately and consistently predicts the direction of the stock market.

Fear of the unknown can cause investors to make poor decisions...or to avoid making financial decisions altogether. When people are frightened, their brains seek certainty when there is none to be found. Trying to invest successfully while simultaneously being afraid to invest renders us paralyzed and exhausted. When we do act, we become our own worst enemies, repeatedly making decisions to buy and sell out of fear, afraid of the unknown. Eventually, we make so many mistakes, we flee to the apparent shelter of the nearest investment with "guaranteed" written on it. Even though the investment doesn't align with our long-term goals, we buy it anyway.

"Nothing in life is to be feared, it is only to be understood. Now is the time to understand more, so that we may fear less."
Marie Curie

A Diamond in the Rough

Our financial future is determined not by what happens to us but by our perceptions and reactions to what happens to us as shown in parable below:

> *A South African farmer grew weary of his arduous daily routine. When he heard tales of other farmers who made great fortunes discovering diamond mines, he sold his farm and spent the rest of his life traveling the African continent in a fruitless search for diamonds. Having found none, depressed and miserable, he threw himself into the ocean and drowned.*
>
> *Some time later, while wading across a creek on the property, the man who bought the land from the farmer's estate saw something shiny beneath the water. Its prism-like reflection caught his eye. He thought it was a crystal and without bothering to examine it further, took the odd-shaped stone home and placed it on the fireplace mantle.*
>
> *A friend, who was visiting sometime later saw the stone, examined it closely and was awestruck. "Do you know what you've found?" the visitor asked excitedly. It was one of the largest diamonds ever discovered in Africa. It turned out his creek bed was full of them, some smaller in size but equally brilliant.*
>
> *The first farmer in the story was living on land that contained a fortune in diamonds, yet he sold the property for pennies on the dollar so he could chase a dream elsewhere. Had he taken the time to learn what diamonds look like in their rough state — and searched his property thoroughly— he would have been rich beyond his wildest dreams.*

If you think of the farmland as a metaphor for the financial markets and economy, you may, at this very moment, be standing in the middle of your acre of undiscovered diamonds without realizing it.

When a recession occurs, the markets — like the farmer's land — may appear to be a barren landscape with little promise of treasure. The media may paint a bleak picture of the economy. When more closely examined, however, there may be lucrative financial opportunities available, hidden below the surface, much like the diamonds in the creek. A negative economic environment often disguises the potential for creating significant wealth. We simply have to approach planning for our future in a new and different way. By changing our perception from one of scarcity and fear to one of opportunity and confidence, we discover a way to recognize value in something that appears valueless to others.

Our brain is wired to seek safety and certainty. When we are fearful it twists our perception, distorts reality and causes us to make poor decisions, much like the hapless farmer who ignored the great wealth lying literally under his feet.

A client, Claire, recently saw her forty-year-old daughter pass away. Claire's surviving daughter — ostensibly wishing to take care of her grieving mother — invited Claire to come and live with her. She accepted and, to her surprise, was shocked at how poorly her daughter managed her personal finances. Having just filed bankruptcy, the daughter needed Claire's money and credit to secure a home mortgage. Claire assumed legal responsibility by cosigning the mortgage and in addition, ended up raising her grandchildren while living in the house. While she enjoyed spending time with her grandchildren, raising her grandchildren at age 68 was not something she was planning on doing. This was the result of making an emotional decision so quickly after the death of her older daughter.

Unlike Claire and the South African farmer, successful investing requires patience and calm. Avoid making major decisions — financial or otherwise — in an environment of sorrow, fear, anger or other emotion. Judgment is clouded and the chances of making a wise decision are minimal.

Chapter Two

Don't Pick the "Right" Stock.
Pick the "Right" (or Left) Brain

*"We too often confront postmodern
dilemmas with an emotional repertoire
tailored to the urgencies of the [ancient]
Pleistocene period."*
Daniel Goleman

Our brain is wired to think the same way it did 50,000 years ago when our ancestors survived by hunting wild animals. If prehistoric man encountered an animal too large or ferocious to contest, his instincts would tell him to run and find a place of refuge, in anticipation of danger.

In the area of the brain called the limbic system, lies the amygdala, the integrative center for emotions, emotional behavior and motivation. When you think of the amygdala, you should think of one word: fear. The amygdala causes us to be fearful of the unknown. It also controls the way we react to certain stimuli, like a situation where we feel threatened or endangered.

Commonly known as the "fight or flight syndrome" that helps us avoid smashing into another car or circumvent potentially dangerous situations, the amygdala is ignited when we experience a financial loss. We are born wired to react to unanticipated events in this way. It can save our life or cause us to make ridiculous errors. We are susceptible anytime fear creeps into our thinking. Our brain reacts to a plunging stock market the same way it reacts to being attacked by a snake. Obviously, this fearful state of mind is not optimal when making decisions about your money.

Uncertainty: The Ultimate Driving Machine

"The brain likes to know what is going on by recognizing patterns in the world. It likes to feel certain...because uncertainty feels like a threat to your life."
David Rock

Allie

The brain, which controls our emotions, works hard at trying to predict the future because it craves certainty. People make plans based solely on weather reports that are frequently inaccurate. Gamblers spend countless hours poring over racing forms or parlay cards trying to predict the future and make winning wagers. Even trying to understand my two-year old son is an exercise in futility.

In his book, *On Intelligence*, Jeff Hawkins says, "Your brain receives patterns in the outside world, stores them as memories and makes predictions by combining what it has seen before and what is happening now."

The average investor consistently makes poor decisions. Dalbar's 2016 Quantitative Analysis of Investor Behavior (QAIB)[1] is the report that examined the returns investors actually realize and the behaviors that produce those returns. The annual report measured the effects of investor decisions to buy, sell and switch into and out of mutual funds over both short and long time frames. The results showed that the average investor earns less — in many cases much less — than mutual fund performance reports would suggest.

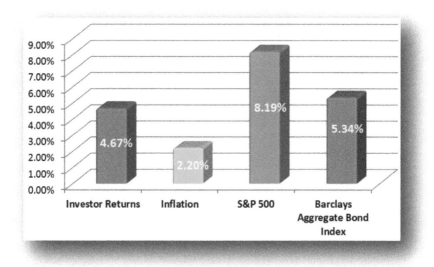

Returns are for the 20 year period ending December 31, 2015. Annualized Investor returns are calculated using the data supplied by the Investment Company Institute and are represented by the change in total mutual fund assets after excluding sales, redemptions and exchanges. The method of calculation captures realized and unrealized capital gains, dividends, interest, trading costs, sales charges, fees, expenses and any other costs. Past performance is no guarantee of future results.

Left Brain vs. Right Brain

We sometimes hear people describe themselves as being either left brained or right brained. It can be instructive to examine this concept as it relates to financial decision-making.

Experimentation has shown that the two different sides, or hemispheres, of the brain are responsible for different manners of thinking. Most individuals have a distinct preference for one of these styles of thinking. Some, however, are equally adept at both modes.[2]

The origin of the right brain-left brain theory is Roger Sperry, who was awarded the Nobel Prize in 1981. Sperry discovered that the two spheres of the human brain perform very different functions. The right brain is visual and processes information intuitively. It's the first to make judgments and decisions. It utilizes first impressions to help keep us out of trouble like avoiding an open manhole. The left brain is verbal and processes information analytically and sequentially. We rely on the intuitive (right) side of our brain to give us a quick assessment of what is happening: If we need more information, the analytical (left) side of our brain supplies it. In her wonderful book, *Awakening the Brain*, author Dr. Charlotte Tomaino says, "the left hemisphere (of the brain) processes the trees and the right hemisphere the forest. In the left hemisphere, we find the details; in the right, the configuration of the details into a whole gestalt."

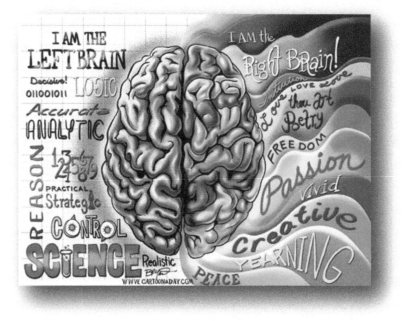

Educational researchers have concluded that learning could proceed at an astounding rate when teachers have students integrate both sides of their brain in a lesson. For example, kindergarten teachers who use music, dance, storytelling, drama, or other right brain activities as part of their routine teaching strategy not only aid the left brain learning of their students, but the students also learn at incredible rates. When the use of these aids diminishes after third grade, learning rates drop significantly.[3]

Nobel laureate Daniel Kahneman describes right brain investing as System 1 (reactionary) decisions in his book, *Thinking Fast and Slow.* "There isn't any deep thinking going on. If an investment sounds good, it must be good. Relying on intuition for investment decisions is a mistake. We are prone to overestimate how much we understand about the world and underestimate the role of chance in events."

Kahneman believes our right brain is incapable of considering risk and return simultaneously and that our left brain must perform the task of analytical thought that the right brain lacks. He calls this System 2 or slow thinking, which is in charge of recognizing and changing the biases inherent in System 1 decisions.

Left brained investors tend to examine the facts before making a choice between risk and return. They look at the past figures and future probabilities, consider overall portfolio construction, fund expenses, turnover, diversification, taxes and other relevant factors. This analytical work may uncover issues with investments that right brained people typically miss.

On the other hand, if you were exclusively left brained, you would be exhausted at the end of the day because of constantly analyzing everything. That's why the right brain can occasionally kick in and come to the rescue, providing an emotional relief from the left brained analysis.

Hastily made decisions by right brained investors often come back to haunt them. They fret over their past mistakes and endlessly speculate about what might happen in the future. But there are no solutions to the failed events of the past or situations that exist in the uncertain future. The present is the only place where solutions can be found. The past can offer insight as to how things might be done differently, but it can also make people angry that they cannot change what has already happened.

It's vital to understand that whether your natural tendency is towards right or left brained thinking, you can learn to control your reactions to what happens, or what you see, hear or interpret from outside sources. It's a matter of finding an appropriate left/right mix.

Unfortunately, many investors rely on the wrong side of their brain to solve a financial problem. Their intuition or "gut" feeling may cause them to make a financial decision that appears to be based on facts but they fail to ask the right question. Kahneman says, "People who are confronted with a difficult question sometimes ask an easier question instead."

There is the story of the Wall Street businessman who attended an exposition of Ford Motor Company's new car models for the coming year. As he observed the vehicles, he became so excited about the cars' styling and innovations that the next day he hastily purchased shares of Ford stock, thinking the stock price would increase in value, without considering whether the shares were *already* fairly valued. The businessman reacted to his right (intuitive) brain by making the purchase so quickly. If this can happen to someone in the business of evaluating stocks, it's easy to see how readily it can happen to the average investor. If the businessman had used his left brain (analytical), he may have realized the stock price had already reflected these new innovations and improvements in style.

Our emotional state of mind plays a crucial role in intuitive decisions and judgments. Kahneman suggests that intuitive judgments are educated guesses where decisions are guided not by deliberation or reasoning but rather by feelings of liking or disliking something. The businessman's decision whether to buy Ford Stock required research and analysis of the future earnings potential of the company. He instead answered the easier question: "Hey, do I love the new Ford automobiles?" He thus relied on the answer to a simplistic (and wrong) question to make a challenging financial decision.

When confronted with a perplexing financial decision, be wary of relying on intuition or hunches. You may inadvertently answer an easier question instead, without noticing you made the switch.

Chapter Three

How You *Think* Can Cause Your Wallet to *Shrink*

Allie

As a young girl, I recall how frightened I would sometimes become after my dad put me to bed and turned out the light. If it were windy outside, I would hear the rustling of the tree branches as they scratched the outside of my bedroom window. The noise would convince me a boogeyman was breaking into my room.

Perception and reality can be completely different things, appearances aside. Our perceptions may convince us we are experiencing reality but they often mislead us.

Have you ever walked along the shore and viewed the horizon on a cloudless day? It looks as though blue water converges with the pristine sky. It's an illusion, a compelling one.

> *"Investors are prone to committing specific errors of which some are minor and others fatal. By allowing psychological bias and emotion to affect their investment decisions, investors can do serious harm to their wealth."*
> Hersh Shefrin

As mentioned earlier, people's primal fears emerge when they invest. The fear of the unknown causes them to make poor decisions, not because of the unknown, per se, but rather because of how they react to it.

Researchers and academics have completed numerous studies on how investors behave and react to what happens in the markets. Referred to as behavioral finance, a great deal has been learned about the impact of investor emotions and biases on financial decision-making.

Behavioral finance research delves into the psychological factors (behavioral biases) that affect investment decisions. Overwhelmingly, the research concludes that certain identifiable biases distort investors' perceptions of information and may cause them to reach incorrect conclusions, even if the information is correct. Their emotions and biases tend to impair their investment judgments.

It's common for investors to stray from what is logical and even what is rational, when evaluating financial information. Emotions, biases and even personality traits can all get in the way of clear thinking. Despite what many people believe — that investing is primarily analyzing data in order to make decisions about buying and selling securities — individual behavior plays a huge role in determining the eventual success or failure of those decisions.

According to researchers Kahneman and Riepe, "Investors who are prone to these biases will take risks they do not acknowledge, experience outcomes they did not anticipate, will be prone to unjustified trading and may end up blaming themselves or others when outcomes are bad."[4]

In this chapter, we will briefly discuss some of the more common biases that affect investor thinking. Some have common characteristics or may appear to overlap but each plays a role in defining how investors perceive and react to financial information and their resulting investment choices.

Confirmation Bias

Confirmation is a behavioral bias that prompts you to embrace information that supports what you already believe. It's a form of selective thinking. It prompts people to place greater emphasis on evidence that corroborates their own beliefs and ignore evidence that disputes them. As a result, their beliefs are reinforced, whether valid or invalid.

People who claim to have seen UFOs are usually adamant about not having any doubts. Confirmation bias causes them to interpret the experience as proof of the existence of alien beings and they typically seek additional data or the affirmation of others claiming a similar experience to reinforce their belief. They ignore evidence to the contrary, even when a logical (and non-interplanetary) explanation for the phenomenon is presented. The tendency to give more weight to what they already believe to be true also influences their memory. When recalling their experiences, they are more likely to recall data that confirms their beliefs.

In a paper written by Aaron T. Beck and Emily A.P. Haigh on Advances in Cognitive Theory and Therapy: The Generic Cognitive Model, they discuss that beliefs influence how people feel and how they act.[5] An example of this is commonly found during an election season. Many voters tend to reaffirm information presented by the media that paints their candidate in a positive way. In addition, they tend to emphasize any negative information related to the opposing candidate.

A confirmation bias can be deadly for investors. A widow refused to liquidate the slumping stock in her retirement portfolio because it was the lifelong favorite of her recently deceased husband. "Frank loved that company and told me it would always do well so I intend to keep it, no matter how poorly it may be performing right now," she asserted.

From an article in the May, 2013 issue of Forbes: "Once an investor starts to like a company, he may dismiss negative information as irrelevant or inaccurate. Investors often stick with a declining stock far longer than they should because they interpret every bit of news about the company in a way that favors the company prospects, and even seek out information that bolsters their case that the company remains a good investment."

Whatever reason you have for making an investment, there's always an opposing reason why you shouldn't. If you listen only to what you already believe or want to hear, the problem becomes even worse after you invest when your confirmation bias causes you to cling stubbornly to your decision.

> *"Confirmation bias is the most effective way
> to go on living a lie."*
> Chriss Jami

Cognitive Dissonance

Cognitive dissonance — a type of confirmation bias — is also a form of self-deception, primarily employed to avoid regret for previous decisions. Investors who buy a stock and then discover they overlooked information that would have discouraged them from making the purchase may discount or ignore the new revelation in order to alleviate the embarrassment of having made a poor choice.

Their brain avoids conflict by discounting new information and seeking additional support for the previously established belief. The tendency is to interpret information in a way that confirms one's preconceptions.

A golfer purchases a new driver after seeing one of his buddies hit the club with great success. But he can't duplicate the result and later learns the club is designed for someone with a much faster swing speed.

Embarrassed by his oversight, he spends the rest of the year flailing away, haplessly trying to make the club work and unwilling to admit his mistake.

While logic suggests that investors will reverse decisions or change behaviors that result in negative consequences, researchers repeatedly see that negative consequences may actually cause investors to *increase* their commitment to a belief and risk continued adverse consequences.[6]

Familiarity Bias

People tend to be more comfortable with what is familiar. This certainly holds true for investors exhibiting a familiarity bias, which causes them to put too much faith in familiar stocks because they believe they are less risky than other, less recognizable stocks.

An example would be investors who over-allocate shares of the company they work for and risk being under-diversified.

The widow of a longtime employee of a large manufacturing company has a retirement portfolio heavily overweighted in stock from her deceased husband's firm. She resists advice to diversify the portfolio and reduce her exposure because her husband often told her the stock was the "safest investment in the world." Her comfort with that stock, despite the obvious danger its over-allocation poses, is a clear example of familiarity bias. In this example, the stock remained at the same price for over 12 years.

> *"Investors are always biased to invest in things they themselves understand."*
>
> Peter Thiel

Home Bias

Investors who own a disproportionate amount of stocks from their own country and ignore the advantages of international diversification are referred to as having a home bias. A major reason for this action is investors are more familiar with companies in their own country. United States companies account for approximately 50% of the global market capitalization. Instead of taking advantage of the ability to invest in countries all over the world, people are fearful of the unknown. Investing in familiar companies feels safer.

Overconfidence

When investors believe they have influence over the outcome of uncontrollable events — often referred to as the illusion of control — they suffer from an overconfidence bias. The vast array of available information can also create an illusion of knowledge among these investors, but more information does not necessarily mean greater knowledge because most investors lack the experience and financial sophistication to apply the information correctly. In addition, investors with an overconfidence bias tend to interpret new information as confirmation of their prior beliefs. This may cause them to trade too much, take too much risk, pay too much in commissions and taxes and be susceptible to big losses.

> *"The illusion that we understand the past fosters overconfidence in our ability to predict the future."*
> Daniel Kahneman

Overconfidence is greatest for difficult tasks, for forecasts with low predictability and for undertakings lacking fast, clear feedback. Selecting stocks that will outperform the market is a difficult task. Predictability is low; feedback is noisy. Thus, stock selection is the type of task for which people are most overconfident.[7]

An example where past success led to overconfidence occurred in 2012 when Kodak filed for bankruptcy. John Kotter, professor emeritus at Harvard Business School, noted that Kodak's failure resulted from complacency bred by its own success. The company had stopped innovating and stopped creating urgency around changes in its marketplace, and, perhaps as damaging, its executives had stopped listening to employees who saw the problems coming. Overconfidence created by success leads to poor decisions.[8]

In 2001, Barber and Odean analyzed the trading activities of people with discount brokerage accounts. They found that the more people traded, the worse they did, on average. Additionally, men traded more and did worse than women investors.[9]

A client asked us to take a look at her mother's Fidelity brokerage account. The mom had forgotten about it for some 15 years and when she and the daughter looked into it, they were pleasantly surprised to find it had done quite well during the years she had ignored it. We researched a bit more and discovered Fidelity had done a study to identify which of their accounts had performed the best over the long term and what were they invested in. The results of the study were quite amazing: the best performing accounts over the long haul belonged to clients who, like our client's mother, had simply forgotten about their accounts and done nothing.[10]

Think about that. The people who achieved the best performance with their accounts were those who forgot they had them!

Writing in the *Harvard Business Review*[11], Jeff Stibel notes, "The future, like any complex problem, has far too many variables to be predicted. Quantitative models, historical models, even psychic models have all been tried — and have all failed. Just imagine predicting something far simpler than the future of the stock market; say, chess. There are an overwhelming 10 to the 120th power possible moves. That's a 1 followed by 120 zeros! As James Hogan explains it in his book *Mind Matters*, that sum far exceeds the number of atoms in the universe."

Stibel mentions that curiously, the one model that appeared to be doing a good job of predicting the stock market at the time was what he dubbed the *Tiger Bears and Bulls Index*. The model tracked Tiger Woods' tournament performance against the Dow. The results were striking: the model predicted virtually every peak and trough of the Dow Industrials average with amazing accuracy from 1993 through 2009 when the article was written.

Of course, given the unfortunate direction of Mr. Woods' health and tournament scores over the past few years, whatever value that model had has now outlived its usefulness.

Despite the overwhelming evidence to the contrary, many investors continue to believe there exists some method of accurately predicting the future direction of the markets.

Self-Attribution

Investors who suffer from self-attribution bias tend to attribute successful outcomes to their own actions while assigning poor outcomes to external factors. They often exhibit this bias as a means of self-protection or self-enhancement. It's the tendency to judge oneself in a positive manner even when the positive evaluation is not justified.

Have you ever watched a professional football player score a touchdown and then put on a display of personal bravado, as if he alone was responsible for the achievement and not the contributions of the other ten players on his team who provided the critical support (blocking) so he could score? That's self-attribution in its purest form.

Interestingly, individuals are not the only investors prone to self-attribution and other emotional biases. Many institutional investors, advisors and other financial professionals are psychologically predisposed to the same biases. Researcher and writer James Montier points out that "Professional investors are just as likely to suffer behavioral biases as the rest of us. Indeed, in as much as they are experts in their field, they may well be even more overconfident and overoptimistic than lay people."[12]

Representativeness

Trying to assess the probability of an event based on assumptions or past experience is called a representativeness bias. It occurs when investors gauge an investment as good or bad based on its recent performance. The typical result is to buy securities after prices have risen — expecting the increases to continue — while overlooking securities with prices below their inherent values.

When investors are unable to fit an event into a defined category, they instead assign it to an organizational system they have already accepted. For example, if most of the celebrity chefs we see on TV are rotund, we tend to generalize that all chefs are overweight.

Representativeness bias causes investors to assign too much emphasis to the recent performance of a stock while undervaluing the stock's long-term averages. Sometimes referred to as the "law of small numbers," an example would be overweighting a portfolio in financial stocks because the sector outperformed the markets during the previous year. It's the notion that what happened most recently is normal and destined to continue.

Do you recall Aesop's fable, *The Goose That Laid the Golden Egg*? It's the story of a married couple with a very special goose that laid a golden egg every day. They became very wealthy but the wife said, "If we could have all the golden eggs that are inside that goose, we could be richer much faster." The husband agreed and so the couple killed the goose and cut her open, only to discover she was just like every other goose. She had no golden eggs inside of her at all.

The lesson is, of course, when you become greedy, you are likely to end up with nothing, something a client, Bobby, finally realized. Bobby became a client in 2003, a couple of years after the technology bubble had burst. We had previously met three years earlier when Bobby had asked me to review his portfolio. Interestingly, it was a portfolio consisting of a single technology fund. He explained that he had liquidated the six other funds in his portfolio and moved all the money into a single tech fund that had been outperforming the other funds. Despite the fact that his fund was doing well, I warned him of the dangers of having all his eggs in one basket, and advised him to diversify into other mutual funds. However, he decided to remain fully invested in the one technology fund. Needless to say, when the tech bubble burst a few months later, his portfolio took a nosedive, along with a lot of other investors who were overweighted in dot.com securities.

The so-called *gambler's fallacy* is another example of Representativeness wherein gamblers erroneously believe that runs in good and bad luck occur. It's actually a misinterpretation of probability, that is, the belief that the odds for something with a fixed probability increase or decrease depending upon recent occurrences. This leads inveterate gamblers to assume they are due for a win after a long string of losses, but the probability of an outcome does not change based on the previous outcomes.

Loss Aversion

The propensity for investors to try to avoid losses — even at the risk of ignoring possible gains — is called loss aversion. It's the tendency to prefer avoiding a loss to receiving a gain. Investors hang onto losing stocks far longer than they should because to sell would be to acknowledge and realize a loss. By not selling, it remains merely a paper loss. This bias helps explain why so many investors repeatedly make the same irrational decisions.

Have you ever gone to a movie and realized you hated it after 30 minutes? Yet you stay parked in your seat for the whole miserable experience rather than getting up and leaving. Something inside you says you paid for the ticket and so you are not going to waste the money.

Interestingly, research has shown that the feeling of losing and gaining the same thing is much different. We would rather choose not to lose over gaining the same thing. In other words, the negative feelings coming from the loss are much stronger than the positive ones coming from the gain. Or to state it more briefly: we simply hate losing. And that creates loss aversion.[13]

According to stress management expert Elizabeth Scott, "When under financial stress, people often experience trouble sleeping, which can add up to a sleep deficit, impairing immune functioning and cognitive abilities. Financial losses are processed in the same area of the brain that responds to mortal danger. We can relive our financial losses in our sleep. This helps explain why losses hurt so much more than gains feel good. Loss aversion can be a huge problem for our long-term financial health if we let the mortal danger signal take over during a panic in the markets."[14]

Roadblock

A roadblock occurs when you base your decision on a personal experience or isolated example instead of empiric evidence or sound reasoning.

An example is the chap who sold his business, netting $1.2 million to provide his retirement income. Years before, he suffered a loss on a stock tip from a friend. That single bad experience convinced him the stock market was unsafe and so he invested the entire $1.2 million in CDs at his bank. His roadblock, created by an isolated event, will now create an even bigger problem: The investment returns on his CDs will barely keep pace with inflation, much less generate the retirement income he needs. He will eventually exhaust his capital, leaving nothing to produce income.

In another instance, a young man saw his parents have their home repossessed. The event was so traumatic as to create a roadblock in his mind about mortgages. Later, when married, he convinced his wife to funnel every extra dollar they had into paying off their mortgage as quickly as possible. The couple was allocating an extra $2,500 a month toward his goal, money that was originally intended for investment in their retirement. When an unexpected contingency arose and the couple needed cash, they were forced to take out an equity loan at an unfavorable interest rate. Instead of having their money earning interest for their retirement, they were now paying interest on it.

Anchoring

When relying on an initial piece of information to make subsequent judgments, it's called an anchoring bias. This is often rooted in the tendency to seek validation. For example, investors may cling to a particular sell price target, even when new information to the contrary is presented. If they can't let go of what they think the sell price should be, they become immobilized.

Anchoring occurs in many decision-making situations, not just choosing investments. It's one reason why marketers establish high opening prices on the goods they sell. It creates an initial value bias in buyers' minds that tends to influence the final price negotiation. So if you see the sticker price of a new BMW is $66,000 and you negotiate a final price of $62,500, you feel you made a good buy because your perception is based on the higher initial price.

An example from psychcentral.com further illustrates the anchoring bias: If a husband is doing ten times more housework than his dad ever did, he may feel entitled to a "best husband of the year" award from his wife. Imagine his surprise then, when his wife berates him for not doing enough. What's going on here is the effect of anchoring. His anchor is what his dad used to do. Her anchor is the amount of housework she does![15]

A common form of anchoring among even highly intelligent or educated people is giving undue weight to early evidence. By accepting early information, they risk creating a bias that distorts their view of any later evidence. Some testing has shown that even when early evidence is later proven to be false, people still retain the original bias and their outlook is continually skewed.

We know of a physician who took a flyer on a penny stock based on something he read while on vacation one summer. The stock soared in value and the physician, believing he had found a "system," spent the next several years trying to duplicate his success. He never did, but despite his unbroken record of losers, he continued to insist his methodology was correct and will eventually be validated.

Attribution

Attribution is assuming our success is due to skill rather than luck. Self-serving attribution takes credit for good outcomes and blames others for bad outcomes.

We have a friend who bought Apple stock in the mid-eighties when it was $15. He bases his stock-picking genius on that decision. It's all he talks about. What he doesn't talk about is during the same period, he also bought ten other stocks, seven of which subsequently plummeted in value. He maintains that he is a great stock picker because he bought Apple. The reason the rest of the stocks went down wasn't his fault; it was because of a bad market. This is an example of the self-serving attribution bias in its purest form.

How can someone be a smart investor if he made mistakes in the past? Instead of remembering the past accurately, our friend chooses to recall only the events that preserve his enhanced self-image.

Regardless of whether brilliance or blind luck, some people believe they can pick stock winners and they continue to try. Being lucky occasionally does not make them an expert, but people with attribution bias cling to the belief that their success was due to financial acumen, not good fortune.

An example of the role luck can play in our lives and our success is the story of Louie Zamperini as detailed in his novel, *Unbroken*.

Zamperini was an Olympic distance runner and World War II bombardier. While searching for a lost aircraft and crew in the South Pacific, his plane crashed, killing eight of the eleven men aboard. Louie and his two mates spent 47 days adrift on a lifeboat, subsisting on rainwater and raw fish.

At one point, a plane flew over and they thought they were rescued, but it turned out to be a Japanese bomber that began strafing the helpless trio. Realizing that bullets are rendered ineffective underwater, Louie got his mates off the boat and into the water to escape the attack. But the three men now faced a new threat: a group of circling sharks. So as the plane flew off, Louie, the most athletic of the three, managed to get the others back into the boat, just in time to face another round of strafing by the bomber. Calling on his physical stamina from years of distance running, Louie repeated the process of getting the men into the water, away from the bullets, and back into the raft to avoid the sharks. Finally, Louie realized he could no longer protect the survivors, so as he lay exhausted on the lifeboat, anticipating the next round of gunfire from the oncoming bomber, the Japanese aircraft dropped a depth charge right next to the raft and waited for it to explode. But nothing happened! Louie's luck had changed. The depth charge didn't explode and amazingly, the bomber gave up and flew off.

Louie was an exceptional athlete and his physical stamina is what saved him and his friends. It's impossible, however, not to recognize the role that luck played in their death-cheating adventure. In his memoirs, Louie later described the event and the role luck played in it.

People like to attribute their investment success to being smart or talented. But if Louie Zamperini, who was physically able to overcome such an unimaginable challenge, could admit the role luck played in his survival, what makes it so difficult for some people to admit that luck is often the reason for the good things that happen in their lives?

In his best-selling book, *Fooled by Randomness: The Hidden Role of Chance in Life and in the Markets,* author Nassim Taleb attributes our perceived success as to being "lucky fools." He further states, "Probability is not a mere computation of odds on the dice or more complicated variants; it is the acceptance of the lack of certainty in our knowledge and the development of methods for dealing with our ignorance."

Mental Accounting

Allie

Mental accounting is the tendency to separate your money based on subjective criteria, such as where the money came from or what you intend to do with it.

A common practice is to maintain separate accounts for different investment objectives. Individuals have been known to save for their children's college education in a bank account paying little interest while paying double-digit interest on purchases made with their credit cards.

Individuals with a mental accounting bias tend to treat money differently depending on where it comes from. An unexpected largesse — such as a gift, casino winnings, inheritance or tax refund — is viewed as *house money* to be spent frivolously. Mental accounting causes people to take risks with that money that they would not take with money they earned working, even though there is no difference.

Mental accounting caused our first father-daughter fight about money. When I was eight years old, I found a $20 bill on the ground and was convinced I was going to buy some candy with it. My dad tried to show me how much money it was (over two weeks of allowance!) but because I had found the money, it became superfluous. I felt I was entitled to spend it frivolously. Evidently, the mental accounting bias can start at a very young age! I probably ended up buying some candy, but in hindsight I should have started my investing days a little sooner. A $20 investment in Apple stock in 1991 would have grown over a hundred-fold over the following 26 years. [16]

Richard Thaler, a behavioral economist at the University of Chicago, first explored the consequences of this irrational behavior. When Thaler asked people whether they would drive 20 minutes out of their way to save $5 on a $15 calculator, 68% said yes. When he asked whether they would drive 20 minutes out of their way to save $5 on a $125 leather jacket, however, only 29% said yes. Their mental accounting identified the percentage of savings as being more important than the money saved, although the amount of savings was identical.

An article in the Washington Post reaffirmed that where money comes from influences how people decide to spend it. It stated that people are more likely to be impulsive or reckless with unexpected money because, they reason, it was never factored into their original financial plans. According to Suzanne Fogel, who heads the marketing department at DePaul University, "The source of the money affects how it is spent." As a graduate student, Fogel waited tables to earn money. She found that she carried around a figure in her head; the amount she wanted to make each day. On a day when she passed that target, any additional income became "free money" — even though that money ought to have been a cushion for the days she did not meet her income target.[17]

A client who inherited a substantial amount from her grandmother felt she should put the money into the bank because her grandmother, who never invested in the markets, kept all her money in a bank savings account. Her mental accounting bias caused the young woman to separate inheritance money from other money because of her emotional attachment to a relative who had passed away.

From a financial perspective, all money has the same value and purchasing power, regardless of where it comes from. Whether you won it playing poker or working a second job, there should be no difference in how you treat the value of your money.

Media Bias

The impact of financial media on individual investor decision-making has been well documented. The media is overrun with superficial financial and investing information and analysis. The relevant information it does report typically arrives too late to be of any real value. By the time an economy is pulling out of recession, reporters are still writing their doom and gloom stories. And reporters are not financial experts; most know little about investing. If the market is up, they rationalize why it is up; if it is down, they offer reasons that purport to explain the decline. Investors who regard this kind of information as valid do themselves a disservice and suffer from media bias.

The financial media's bias may, however, be the result of giving investors what they want. A 2011 study by Shengle Lin[18] indicates there is a strong correlation.

According to Lin's research, the financial media has a continuing coverage bias toward stocks that have generated high returns in the past and top performing stocks get far more coverage than underperformers. Lin believes the media's proclivity to cover past winners is driven primarily by an audience seeking information that supports their previous investment decisions.

"Television is chewing gum for the eyes."
Frank Lloyd Wright

It's Not Hopeless

It's hard to overemphasize the impact emotional biases have on individuals, financial markets and economies in general. The root cause of the financial crisis that erupted in 2008 was psychological, according to Shefrin: "In the events that led up to the crisis, the effects of psychological biases strongly influenced the judgments and decisions of financial firms, rating agencies, elected officials, government regulators and institutional investors."[19]

We are all unique in how we process information and make financial decisions. We all have innate emotional biases of one kind or another. Don't let the long list discussed here discourage you. While you can't avoid all biases, you can reduce their effects if you recognize which biases influence your thinking and learn to minimize their impact on your attitude and financial decision-making. In coming chapters, we will discuss techniques to help you overcome your psychological biases and find balance in your emotions and your life.

"Be able to recognize when you're reading or hearing material biased to your own side."
Marilyn vos Savant

Chapter Four

Parents Don't Always Know Best

We have a friend, Steve Zimmer, who has been an NFL referee for many years. He always has some interesting stories to share about his experiences with football players and the dynamics of being a referee in such a fast moving game. Chatting with him during the offseason, we mentioned how difficult it must be to make instantaneous judgments on plays that last only a few seconds.

Steve said that much of it has to do with the type of play he expects will take place as well as his proximity to the play. Why the proximity? It has to do with being the *optimal distance* from what is happening during the play. If you are too close to the action, it becomes a blur. Your view is obscured by the speed of the players' movements and it's difficult to determine if an infraction has been committed. Being a bit farther away — the optimal distance as Steve calls it — makes it easier because the movement slows down and you can see the big picture.

It later struck us that there is an optimal distance when it comes to your money as well. If you are too close to your investment portfolio — hovering over it and tweaking it every day — you get a distorted perspective. Changes can appear very abruptly and clarity becomes difficult. By taking the time to distance yourself from the situation you allow your brain to see the big picture.

"Change the way you look at things and the things you look at change."
Wayne Dyer

Childhood Influences

Walter

After observing people and the problems they have with money over the years, I've come to realize that most financial decisions have less to do with money and more to do with people's perception and beliefs **about** money. Much of that stems from their childhood since their concept of money is formed early on. As adults, those concepts become more emotionally charged and behaviorally imbedded into their consciousness.

How did you learn the value of a dollar? Were you given the opportunity to earn an allowance by doing chores when you were a child? What we were taught as children tends to stay with us into adulthood. Often, people are unaware that they have unconsciously retained childhood observations about money.

We have a friend who is married with three children. Her parents, who paid for everything she needed or wanted since childhood, continued to pay her credit card bills and even a portion of her mortgage after her marriage. It was only recently, when her father began to worry about his finances in retirement that he was forced to cut her off financially. She was upset that he did so "cold turkey" as she put it, but realized he was worried about his own financial future. She failed to change her spending habits and without her father's generosity, she quickly ran up credit card bills. She is now deeply in debt and receiving threatening notices from lenders. She and her husband can no longer afford their luxury home without her parents' help. They must now try to sell it in a weak market and then move their family to a more affordable location. Her situation may not have been as dire had she had acquired a healthier attitude about money at an early age.

We have encountered families where one or more of the children inherited their parents' prudent attitudes about money while others acquired a wasteful, tunnel vision when it came to finances. Usually, children's brains are likely to develop with the same money mentality as their parents.

Financial decisions are really decisions about life, usually based on what we were taught as children and how our brains developed. If, however, our financial perspective is driven by biases or destructive behaviors not aligned with our financial goals, it can be especially difficult to step back and see the big picture. Depending on what is going on in our heads, we may hurt, more than help, ourselves.

©Glasbergen

"...and *that's* why you need to raise my allowance!"

Raising Financially Smart Kids

In many families, frank discussions about money are as taboo as talks about sex or politics. And yet, people who include their children (at an appropriate age) in collaborative money discussions often discover they have imbued not only valuable knowledge but also a healthier attitude about finances in general.

New York Times columnist Ron Lieber has written a wonderful book titled, The Opposite of Spoiled: Raising Kids Who Are Grounded, Generous, and Smart About Money. In it, he details a story about Scott Parker, who grew up in a family that did not discuss money. Scott was therefore determined his kids would have a different experience.

Scott went into a Wells Fargo branch near the family's San Diego home and asked to withdraw his monthly paycheck of around $12,000, all in $1 bills. It took a couple of days for the bank to gather all the singles and stack them into $100 piles.

Scott, who worked in real estate, brought the stacks home and laid them on the dining room table without comment. "I definitely had their attention," he recalled.

He then started peeling singles away from the stacks. First came the family's 10 percent tithe. Income taxes were next, followed by the mortgage and insurance payments. Then came the electric bill, car payments, gas, groceries and other necessities. And those were just the *needs*—the baseline costs that were *not* optional. Next came their money for their weekly restaurant outing, followed by soccer and debate team trips and other activities. By the end of the presentation, there wasn't much money left at all.

"The first thing I thought they might think was that I made a lot of money, because they were sitting there with their mouths open the whole time," he explained. "But that was the last thing I was trying to teach. None of them, I was sure, had ever tried to add any of these things up. So I think it made a strong impression. I probably should have done it again later when the younger kids were older."

Their oldest son, Daniel, remembers many details from that night and also recalls the lengths his father went to explain to the kids that it was a family discussion and therefore nobody needed to tell their friends about it. "I was taking a risk," Parker said, "but I can tell you that it never became an issue. I figured that whatever risk there was that they would talk about it was worth taking."

Walter

As a father of three children and an experienced financial advisor, it is very difficult trying to teach your kids the value of a dollar. Sometimes, they really do think that money grows on trees. All parents should try to find and implement effective strategies in helping your children become more responsible.

Allie

Despite growing up in the same house with the same parents, my brother and I developed surprisingly different perspectives on how to handle money. I guess our brains were wired quite differently.

As children, our allowance was based on our age. When I was 8, my allowance was $8 a week, and so on. We were required to allocate our allowance: 40% spending money, 30% short term savings, 20% long term savings and 10% to help someone in need or to charity.

Looking back on it, it's fascinating how spending and saving habits develop at such a young age. My brother saved everything. We dubbed his room "The Museum." It looks pretty much the same today as the day he left for college, eleven years ago. There are piles of "collectibles" everywhere: pogs, trolls, old soccer trophies, even two dollar bills taped to his wall. There's probably still some Halloween candy from the 1990's in there as well! He was — and is — a consummate saver.

I was less frugal. I spent my money pretty easily although I still managed to save the required 20%. As we got older, the four ratios sort of fell to the wayside, but the concept of savings stayed with us. When we were teenagers, everything we made — whether from a summer job or our birthday checks from grandma — saw 20% go into long-term savings. Our brains developed differently when it came to money but to this day at least, we both remain dedicated savers. Growing up, I'm not sure either of us found the *optimal distance* when it came to handling our finances, but my parents did a great job of teaching us the value of money and the importance of saving.

The beliefs and attitudes you hold in your mind determine what happens in your life, not the other way around. Many people get this backwards. They never come to realize that their life will mirror what goes on inside their brain. The only way to change your relationship with money is to change your mindset. Once you do, the world around can change in response to your new attitude.

> *"Life is not happening to you.*
> *Life is responding to you."*
> Author Unknown

A Cambridge University study suggests that by age seven, most young children have grasped all the main aspects of how money works and formed core behaviors that they will take into adulthood and that will affect financial decisions they make during the rest of their lives.

Dr. David Whitebread, a developmental cognitive psychologist and co-author of the study, said: "The *habits of mind* which influence the ways children approach complex problems and decisions, including financial ones, are largely determined in the first few years of life. Simply imparting information is now recognized as being ineffective in this area.

By contrast, early experiences provided by parents, caregivers and teachers which support children in learning how to plan ahead, in being reflective in their thinking and in being able to regulate their emotions, can make a huge difference in promoting beneficial financial behavior."[20]

Money, Family and Stress

People's perception of money can be a significant cause of stress and anxiety. According to a 2014 survey by Harris Poll on behalf of the American Psychological Association, 72% of Americans identify money as a significant cause of stress in their lives.

Stress over money among parents can have a profound effect on their children. A 2015 T. Rowe Price study, *Parents, Kids & Money Survey* found that parents have just as tough a time talking money with their kids as they do teaching them about sex. One-third of parents reported that they completely avoid conversations with their children about money. 77% of parents said they aren't always honest with their kids about money and 43% report being dishonest about how worried they are about money. This is because parents frequently fail to realize what a meaningful and long-lasting impact the way they deal with money has on their children.

Perception and Reality

Allie

Joy, a friend of mine, was humiliated when she was laid off from her job. Her marketing firm had two rounds of layoffs and she was a casualty of round two. Thankfully, the company gave her three months of severance, but Joy couldn't get over her feelings of inadequacy and wallowed in self-pity. It wasn't until Joy went to dinner with friends, a month later, that she was finally able to open up and talk about it.

Joy admitted that since being fired, she felt emotionally paralyzed and consequently spent the month parked on her living room couch watching TV. She had only recently begun sending out resumes. During dinner she seemed somewhat relieved, and her embarrassment was mitigated. By the time dessert came, she had become motivated to aggressively tackling her job search.

I reconnected with Joy a couple of weeks later. A spot had opened up at a prestigious marketing firm in Manhattan: a dream job at her dream company. Joy went through three rounds of interviews and eventually landed the position with a month of severance money still left in her bank account.

Psychotherapist Dr. Kate Levinson says, "It's important to talk with others, to not let the shame of the situation or the self-criticism stop you from getting support. Talking with others not only helps us to problem-solve, but also to feel not so alone and isolated in handling the situation. To go through this problem with other people absolutely brings a better outcome."[21]

Joy's story is just one of many during the period when the economy slumped in response to the 2008 market crash. In some instances, my friends didn't find new jobs right away. A few moved back with their parents (the horror!) or borrowed money to live until they could get back on their feet. Others had enough in their savings to last them a few months before they decided to pick up and move to a different part of the country to start over. All of them had to overcome obstacles that challenged whether they were tough enough to get through it and move on. Amazingly, every one of my friends whose position was downsized ended up finding new employment and today is happier than before. The period of time without a job forced them into some tough decisions but ultimately it gave them time to think about the person they wanted to become and the direction they wanted their lives to take.

"We are all faced with a series of great opportunities brilliantly disguised as impossible situations."
Charles Swindoll

Opportunities often disguise themselves and emerge in the strangest places. What may appear to be a terrible setback can lead you towards a happier place in life. Bad things happen to everyone at one time or another. However, it's not what happens to you in life; it's how you perceive and react to what happens that determines whether you are weakened or empowered.

Chapter Five

The Magic of Music and the Science of Synchronicity

"In the end we shall have had enough of cynicism, skepticism and humbug, and we shall want to live more musically."
Vincent van Gogh

Allie

It was my two year old son Cooper's bedtime and we were waiting for my husband, Scott, to get home from work. I decided to keep Cooper up until Scott arrived since it was only a few extra minutes. We spent the time listening to music and relaxing on the couch together. As soon as I turned on the music, I noticed a difference in Cooper's demeanor. He became calmer, almost mesmerized and his breathing became deeper. The transformation into this peaceful state of tranquility was pretty amazing. I'm sure a little bit of his peacefulness had to do with it being bedtime, but I couldn't help but notice a change at the exact moment the music started playing.

Walter:

When I was a child I studied classical piano, hoping to someday become a concert pianist. In preparation for a performance, I would play classical pieces for patients in nursing homes and couldn't help but notice how the music seemed to elevate their spirits. Many years later, my mother suffered from symptoms of dementia and eventually became a patient in one of these facilities. I would go there to play and sing her favorite songs from the 1930s and 1940s, even though it was apparent she no longer remembered me. But on one occasion, I played a song called "Take Me Back to New York Town," a favorite of hers when she was a little girl. As I played and sang, she looked at me and I noticed a momentary flicker of recognition and then she began to sing along. The music evidently awakened a memory that had been rendered dormant from the disease. That's when I became aware of the effects music has on the brain.

Soon after, I became involved with *Music and Memory*, a non-profit organization dedicated to bringing personalized music into lives of the elderly and infirmed. In 2006 an idea struck director Dan Cohen: if he ended up in a nursing home, he wanted to be able to listen to his favorite 60s music. The nascent popularity of iPods triggered his intention to bring them into nursing homes to provide personalized music for residents. His efforts were an immediate hit with residents and staff alike, and became the prototype for a larger effort.

With funding from the Shelley & Donald Rubin Foundation in 2008, Dan brought 200 iPods to residents of four New York long-term care facilities and tested the program on a larger scale. Successful outcomes spurred the creation of *Music & Memory* in 2010.[22]

I've personally witnessed the improved quality of life that music brings to nursing home residents, especially those with Alzheimer's disease. Although patients with dementia might no longer recognize their family or even be able to speak, they come alive when listening to familiar music from their youth. Working with nursing home staff members, we recruited local high school students to contact the families of patients to learn what kind of music resonated with them. The students then downloaded the music onto iPods and gave them to the patients as gifts.

I have been so moved by the inspiring effects of music on previously unresponsive patients that I have dedicated time to making it easier for patients in nursing homes to have access to iPods. As a member of the local Rotary Club, I was able to sponsor a program to purchase iPods for the nursing home patients. Music improves their quality of life by organizing their thoughts and calming their demeanor, especially in the late afternoon as they are preparing to sit for their evening meal. Interestingly, I find I can apply much of what I learned in my interaction with the nursing home patients to my financial planning practice; specifically the positive effect of music on emotions and behavior in financial decision-making.

> *"The mind has a powerful way of attracting things that are in harmony with it, good and bad."*
> Idowu Koyenikan

The Phenomenon of Synchronicity

In the late 1600s, there was a Dutch physicist named Christian Huygens, who invented the pendulum clock and was a renowned scientist on the subject of timekeeping. One day, upon close observation of two of his clocks hanging on a wall, Huygens noticed something odd: No matter how the pendulums on the clocks were set in motion, within a half-hour or so they would swing in exactly the same direction as one another. Huygens referred to the phenomenon as an "odd kind of sympathy." What he actually discovered was that everything in nature wants to synchronize.

It was not until 2015 that someone was able to explain this phenomenon. Scientist Henrique Oliveira and University of London physicist Luís Melo calculated that as pendulums move back and forth, the vibrating sound waves, similar to the sound waves and beats of music, travel through the wall from clock to clock. The pulses alter the swings of the pendulums, eventually causing them to synchronize.

Such synchronicity exists in many areas, not just between clocks. We acquire emotional energies throughout our lives. We are physically and biologically wired to want to move harmoniously with others. Our bodies want to generate a calm, organized feeling. You can find it in music, medicine, sports, mass marketing and even among couples in love.

University of California Davis psychology professor Emilio Ferrer conducted a study on 32 couples in romantic relationships. Each couple sat a few feet apart from one another in a quiet, calm room where they were not allowed to speak or touch. When connected to monitors measuring heart rates and respiration, Ferrer discovered each couple's heart rates were in sync and they breathed in and out at the same intervals. He noted, "We've seen a lot of research that one person in a relationship can experience what the other person is experiencing emotionally, but this study shows they also share experiences at a physiological level."

In a 2002 study of retail shoppers, Michael Morrison reports, "Music can be a powerful emotional stimulant within a retail environment and a valuable primary element in creating or enhancing the sensory experiences of shoppers. Music is versatile; it can relax or excite. Music can subliminally influence shoppers from the moment they step through the door by entertaining, inspiring and motivate. Music can have an influence on potential sales by increasing "shopping" time for both the active and passive shopper and by slowing down the pace of travel throughout the store (Kellaris and Kent, 1992). The right music is thought to have the potential to increase sales opportunities, define retail image and attract more customers."[23]

There are even studies proving that the use of music aids in the recovery of post-surgery patients. Claudius Conrad is a Harvard Medical School surgeon who holds doctorates in both stem cell biology and music philosophy. An accomplished classical pianist who trained in elite music schools in Germany and Austria, Dr. Conrad believes music and medicine are intertwined. While performing heart surgery, he finds listening to Mozart on his iPod beneficial *because it helps keep him in flow.* In addition, Dr. Conrad has conducted studies that indicate music helps reduce blood pressure, heart rate, stress hormones and pain for his post-surgical patients. Those who were exposed to the music of Mozart during recovery had less need for pain medication.

In a paper published December 2016 in the journal Critical Care Medicine, Dr. Conrad and colleagues revealed an unexpected element in distressed patients' physiological response to music: a jump in pituitary growth hormone, which is known to be crucial in healing. "It's a sort of quickening," he said, "that produces a calming effect."[24]

This connection between synchronicity and music should come as no surprise. It's a natural phenomenon. Synchronicity is ubiquitous because it is intertwined with so many of our activities and choices. When we meet with clients in our office to share ideas on financial planning or investment strategy, we quickly become synchronized with one another, much like the clocks. We have calming music playing in the background, which allows their heart rates and blood pressure to slow down, similar to Dr. Conrad performing surgery or the couples in the experiment study. The synchronicity created within this environment helps our clients reduce stress, organize their thoughts, and ultimately gain more control over emotions and behaviors and their relationship with money.

I may be helping to bring harmony between
people through my music.
Nat King Cole

We've had many clients tell us about the impact the concept of synchronicity had on their lives, or about going through a trauma or a tragedy and being able to regain control. We equate the concept of synchronicity to the definition of flow by Mihaly Csikszentmihalyi, the Hungarian psychologist who has extensively studied the pursuit of happiness. He defines flow as, "A state in which people are so involved in an activity that nothing else seems to matter; the experience is so enjoyable that people will continue to do it even at great cost, for the sheer sake of doing it."[25]

A client of ours experienced this concept in college where he was a member of the swim team. He mentioned doing laps for 20 minutes would help him feel calm and in control. Later, when he was going through a difficult divorce, he would go to the local pool every day and swim laps. When he got out of the pool he felt like he could handle the stress of the divorce; he felt in control of his life. *That's synchronicity and flow.* It's gaining control of one's emotions during difficult circumstances.

Similar to the dementia patients who respond to familiar music from their past, perhaps it was the repetitive sound and feel of the water's movement as he swam, which brought back the sense of calm and control to our client. We believe gaining control can result from any activity in which you're *fully* engaged and *nothing else seems to matter.* You might find it on a golf course, fishing in a stream, sailing, or just being outside with the sun shining or the breeze blowing.

One of our consultants remarked that when she was confused or felt conflicted about something, she would go on a long walk with her two big dogs. It cleared her mind and kept her from making a rash or imprudent decision. The walk took her mind off the issue for a while and let her subconscious help bring clarity and insight to her decision.

Tragedy Averted

Walter

A client asked us to provide some financial planning assistance to his sister Heather, who was going through a difficult divorce. There were four children and considerable assets. She was not financially sophisticated and was intimidated by her husband, Steve. My client was worried about the settlement agreement drawn up by Steve's attorney.

I went to visit Heather the next day. While sitting together in her kitchen, I reviewed the settlement and it was obvious that the agreement leaned heavily in her husband's favor. When asked about it, she said despondently, "I don't care anymore about the agreement; I'm afraid he will stop making mortgage payments and I will lose my house. I am so afraid of being thrown out into the street."

I suggested she hire her own attorney to review the document but she refused: "I just want to get this whole thing over with." I sensed her fear and the emotional trauma she was going through, but I was concerned she was making a hasty decision which she would come to regret. I suggested that it's never a good idea to make decisions when emotionally charged and proposed she take a day or two off. I directed her to put the agreement aside and do something that would release her from her frustration.

As I observed her surroundings I noticed there were many crocheted items on display in her home. I asked if the handiwork were hers. She brightened up and said it was her passion and that crocheting provided her with much needed relaxation and satisfaction. However, she had stopped crocheting because of the demands of the children and the demise of her marriage.

I explained that one of the best ways to reduce stress and feel in control was to get into what psychologist Mihaly Csikszentmihalyi called a state of "flow" where nothing but the activity seemed to matter.

Heather took my advice and spent the next day in a state of flow crocheting. She called to tell me she felt so much better after she relaxed and did some crocheting that she was now ready to make some decisions with less emotion involved. We met with my attorney and crafted a settlement that was more favorable for all parties. She agreed that the worst thing she could have done was to make an important decision about money in her previous emotional state of mind, a decision that she would regret afterwards, because as she put it, "I was not thinking with my head on."

When forced to make important decisions that involve the direction of our life, it's wise to first engage in an activity that detaches us from the stress and where nothing else seems to matter.

Heather decided she would like to be more in control of her life. She came to realize that the divorce was not the end, but could be a new beginning for her. Crocheting worked for her the same way music worked for me when I sat at the piano. The feeling of my fingers on the piano keys was just like the sense of control her crocheting gave her.

Similarly, the nursing home patients experienced a life change because the music set them free. There was no disorder or impatience. There was only the music that brought back the memories of who they once were. When they heard the songs, they came alive! They danced and celebrated.

The feeling that the nursing home patients experience is the same feeling you have when engaging in an activity you love that detaches you from the world around you. The magic of music and the science of synchronicity are at work!

"Synchronicity holds the promise that if we will change within, the patterns in our outer life will change also."

Jean Shinoda Bolen

Chapter Six

Your Best Investment: Yourself!

*"If a person gets his attitude toward money
straight, it will help straighten out almost
every other area in his life."*
Reverend Billy Graham

One of the major benefits of changing your perspective on money is
that it allows you to take better control of your life. Changing your
perspective helps you to fully access your personal *human capital*, a
critical step in overcoming your emotional and behavioral biases, and
finding fulfillment.

Your personal finances are divided into four categories:

- Cash savings and money in the bank;
- Invested assets, including 401(k) and brokerage accounts;
- Use Assets, such as your homes, vehicles, jewelry and art; and
- Human Capital.

Human capital defines your ability to be productive and grow. It's
your power to produce. You earn money from a job, profession or
business, but what is that job doing for you? Do you enjoy your work? Is

there potential for personal and financial growth? What are you doing with the money you earn? You pay your bills, expenses and taxes; there is some discretionary spending; hopefully, you save something for the future. If you make $100,000 a year, *a million dollars* will pass through your fingertips over the next 10 years! How you use it to spend, save or pay taxes is largely up to you.

Human capital is the category often overlooked when assessing a person's personal financial picture because it's a dimension not easily defined or measured with numbers.

Many people do not realize that they are in control of their own human capital, earnings potential, and the power to produce money over their working lifetime.

Many young professionals are coming to us early on in their careers. They may have negative net worth because their student loans are greater than their total assets. Though they are able to save only a small amount right now, we enjoy helping them recognize and eventually maximize their financial potential, in turn helping them fulfill their human capital.

We recently discovered an interesting dichotomy between two new clients. One is a man in his mid-fifties who received an inheritance a few years ago. He no longer works, relying on his inheritance portfolio and income from family-managed real estate holdings to meet his expenses. His current total net worth is a bit over a million dollars.

The other client is a pediatric emergency care physician who works long hours in a group practice. She is in her early thirties, is still paying off her student loans and owns no real estate. She earns $300,000 annually but lives frugally and has begun saving $5,000 monthly in an investment account. Her total net worth is negative due to her loans but as her income rises, she will continue to save monthly for her future. We estimate that she will be able to pay off her student loans and hopefully reach millionaire status by age 45, while continuing to grow her net worth for many years to come. In both cases, these clients are millionaires. However, our concern with the first client is that he is not saving into his portfolio. There is a lack of human capital, and the effects of taxes and inflation may have a greater impact on the first client than the young doctor.

So much of our happiness is tied to our financial perspective. Human capital is more powerful than winning the lottery or receiving a windfall inheritance. Start thinking of yourself as an investable asset and consider what you are doing to build and protect this important asset.

> *The greatest money making idea you will ever have is to invest in yourself!*

When you're in the early stages of your career, you may not be making much money, but what career path are you creating for yourself? Your *network of resources* is an important aspect of your human capital. Are you taking advantage of it? Are you marketing yourself, putting yourself out there? Who are you speaking to about your future career? Whose wisdom do you seek? If you have chosen good mentors, do you know what questions to ask them? How did they become successful? What was the catalyst that launched *their* careers?

Some companies have a mentoring program to help younger employees recognize opportunities for growth and determine how they see themselves positioned within the firm. Have you explored that possibility?

In short, accessing your human capital network is about leveraging your career, learning what opportunities might exist in your current position, and attempting to enhance your earnings potential by facilitating a promotion.

Allie

My sister Kim formally held a job at ESPN, accepting an entry-level sales position after graduating college. Every Friday the junior sales associates and the senior managers would gather in the conference room to discuss industry trends and strategic goals. The associates were seated around the perimeter of the room and the managers were seated at the conference room table. The culture of the meetings was predictable: the associates did not speak unless spoken to, they merely listened and took notes and the managers came up with the ideas and action items. On one particular day, there was a request for a research project regarding the television ads of a network competitor. The associates sat looking nervously at one another until my sister spoke up. She volunteered to work on the project and was expected to bring in all of the research and educate the crew at the next team meeting. Her colleagues were afraid of speaking up and possibly exposing their inexperience in their role, but Kim looked at the project as an opportunity to promote her efforts. She now had the wherewithal to work with a Senior Vice President who previously barely knew her name, and now she would be working alongside him gaining valuable insight and guidance. A few months later a position opened up and all the associates were vying for the promotion. My sister Kim, having already made the relationship with the Senior Vice President of sales was one of the first employees to be considered for the role and she was ultimately offered the position!

In this particular situation, my sister had the same level of experience as everyone else. But, she seized the opportunity to make herself stand out. She volunteered her time and energy to a project that was in addition to her normal responsibilities as a junior associate. Everyone has the same capacity to create more human capital. What are *you* doing to tap into this powerful resource?

Walter

The late Wayne Dyer had a marvelous metaphor about never letting what's happened in the past prevent you from creating your best future.

He suggested that in order to recognize the past for what it is, imagine you are standing on the stern of a boat moving through the water. As you stand there, three questions come to mind.

First, what is the wake? The wake is nothing more than the trail left behind by the boat.

Second, what drives the boat? The *present moment energy* you generate through the engine drives the boat.

Finally, is it possible for the wake to propel the boat? Of course not. The wake is a trail left behind. It can never drive the boat.

Now imagine that the boat is your life, and the wake is all the things that have happened in the past — what your parents were like, where you were in the birth order, how your mother treated you, whether your father was an alcoholic, your body shape or anything else.

Most people live with the illusion that their wakes are "driving" their life — which is wrong and, in fact, impossible. In order to nourish your soul, you must be able to take control of the boat and make your own wake.

I think Wayne's analogy is relevant when it comes to organizing our money because, like the wake of a boat, we leave a trail of past financial decisions behind us, both positive and negative. We cannot let that trail drive our financial boat. We must drive the boat. When we are in control, we can command the course, speed and direction of the boat and we are not distracted by the wake.

Taking Control

We recently met with Mary, a client whose husband passed away suddenly. The unforeseen tragedy left Mary dazed and unprepared to make all the financial decisions. After months of grieving, she was finally able to deal with her loss and her newfound financial responsibilities. We reviewed her assets and liabilities, including a rental property the couple had purchased 25 years earlier. It had significantly appreciated in value and generated consistent monthly income. Mary's husband had handled most of the repairs.

We subsequently discussed a plan to invest her husband's assets and life insurance proceeds, representing more than half of her net worth. Mary wanted to pursue a business opportunity involving a lifelong hobby so we developed a plan to diversify her investment portfolio so she could follow her passion. But Mary insisted on purchasing another rental property similar to the one she already owned. She was convinced she could replicate the first property's positive experience.

Like the wake of the boat, she was letting a past experience drive her present decision. She couldn't see how the circumstances had changed from 25 years ago but they had. The area is now in an economic downturn and saturated with rental properties. In addition, her husband is no longer around to do the repairs.

Mary has been presented with an opportunity. She can take control and make a decision based on factors that are relevant to her life today, or she can mimic an experience from 25 years ago and hope for the best.

How can Mary best invest in herself? What is the best use of her Human Capital?

When we unleash the potential of our human capital, we harness the ability to take control of our lives and propel our boat in whatever direction we choose.

"We are products of our past, but we don't have to be prisoners of it."
Rick Warren

Chapter Seven

Enliven Your Optimism, Increase Your Luck

"Some luck lies in not getting what you thought you wanted but getting what you have, which once you have it you may be smart enough to see is what you would have wanted had you known."
Garrison Keillor

People who recognize opportunity and seize it create their own luck. Where others see problems they see possibilities. When things don't work out the way they plan, it is easy for them to move past the disappointment and start looking for the next opportunity. These people are happier and enjoy consistently good luck. They think of themselves as fortunate.

Richard Wiseman, a psychologist from the University of Hertfordshire, England and author of *The Luck Factor*, spent a decade researching people's perceptions of their luck. He found that those who call themselves lucky are more likely to have a fortuitous encounter because they meet lots of new people and keep in touch with a large group of friends and acquaintances. They are also less likely to experience negative emotional states such as anxiety, anger, guilt and depression.

Writing in the *Skeptical Inquirer* in 2003, Wiseman talks about his experience relating to luck, working with volunteers who considered themselves either exceptionally lucky or unlucky. "Over the years I have interviewed these volunteers, asked them to complete diaries, personality questionnaires, and intelligence tests, and invited them to my laboratory to participate in experiments. The findings have revealed that luck is not a magical ability or the result of random chance. Nor are people born lucky or unlucky. Instead, although lucky and unlucky people have almost no insight into the real causes of their good and bad luck, their thoughts and behavior are responsible for much of their fortune."

Writing in *Inc. Magazine*, Peter Economy (yes, that's really his name!) notes that, "Optimistic people naturally create lots of good luck. Studies have proven that more than 80 percent of people who feel they're lucky actually work harder at creating their good luck. On the flip side, people who feel unlucky tend to believe that bad luck just happens to them and that it isn't something they have any power to change. Lucky people view the world with optimism. When bad things happen, it is their optimism that makes them resilient. They are able to pick themselves up and face another day — creating more good luck."[26]

Want to improve your luck? It could be as easy as adjusting your attitude. Studies show that people who consider themselves lucky actually tend to be lucky — it's a self-fulfilling prophecy. That's because positive thinkers are always keeping their eyes peeled for fortuitous situations, and they're more likely to pounce on them when they arise.[27]

If you believe that success in life is outside your control and depends mainly on random chance, you may be inclined to make less effort in pursuing your career ambitions. You may feel, "What's the point? You can make all the effort in the world, but if you're not lucky it won't make a difference."

This way of thinking is a form of what is known in psychology circles as *learned helplessness*. If you believe that things are outside your control and that your actions will not make a difference, you make less effort. If you make less effort, you will be less successful and this will just confirm your belief that you can't change anything.[28]

Bill Gates attributed his achievements to constant striving for improvement more than to luck. "When I was young, I got to use computers. That was very lucky. Then I got to work at a computer company where, because I was pretty good, these senior people looked at my code and told me, 'No, that's not as good as it can be,' and so I got better. And then I had another experience where a great developer looked at my code and told me how to do it better."

Many other young people had the similar luck of using computers in those early years but they didn't come close to achieving Bill's level of success. Obviously, luck was not the differentiator. The difference was that Bill got good at it, kept improving, and took it further than the others, regardless of the luck he had. Success is not determined by this thing called luck, over which we have no control. Success is the result of doing things that we *do* have control over.[29]

Michael Mauboussin, author and head of Global Financial Strategy at Credit Suisse notes, "There is actually a very interesting test to determine if there is any skill in an activity, and that is to ask if you can lose on purpose. If you can lose on purpose, then there is some sort of skill. Investing is very interesting because it is difficult to build a portfolio that does a lot better than the benchmark. But it is also actually very hard, given the parameters, to build a portfolio that does a lot worse than the benchmark. What that tells you is that investing is pretty far over to the luck side of the continuum."

Anthony DeMello, author, Jesuit priest and psychotherapist, tells of a rabbi who worked hard his whole life and finally reached retirement. He prayed to God each day to help him win the lottery. Exasperated after months of praying, he finally blurted out in desperation: "God, please give me a break"! Out of the billowing clouds in the sky he heard God retort, "Give me a break yourself; why don't you buy yourself a lottery ticket!"

We all know people who complain about not being as *lucky* as others. Psychologist Wiseman offers the example of the single woman who would choose a color before attending any party. At the party, she would make it a point to speak to everyone wearing that color, systematically forcing herself to talk to others. She realized that by forcing herself to be outgoing and friendly she would meet people who could create more opportunities to advance her career, not to mention possibly getting asked out on more dates!

Robert Woodward's Story

In 1970, a young lieutenant named Robert Woodward was an assistant to a navy admiral. He was an ambitious twenty seven-year old who would soon be finished with his tour in Vietnam and was eager to start a career in the private sector. He was given instructions to hand deliver a package to the chief of naval operations, but when he arrived, the officer wasn't there so Robert had to wait. After a while, he was joined by an older man who had the persona of someone important and was not interested in making chit chat with an inexperienced naval officer.

Ambitious though he was, Robert hesitated to attempt conversation with the man, but he overcome his reticence, made eye contact and started a conversation. He could tell the older man did not want to engage in a lengthy discussion and just as he was about to give up, the man asked Robert where he attended college. It turned out they both attended George Washington University in Washington D.C., although some thirty years apart. The conversation immediately grew livelier and the two chatted for some time until the chief of staff returned. The older gentleman turned out to be Mark Felt, a senior executive with the Federal Bureau of Investigation. He told young Robert to stay in touch and that if he could help him further his career he would be happy to do so.

After his naval tour ended, Robert landed a job at the Washington Post working as a reporter. When he and Carl Bernstein were later assigned to cover the Watergate scandal, it was Mark Felt, the anonymous "Deep Throat," who became his clandestine source of information that ultimately brought down the presidency of Richard Nixon.

Robert Woodward had no idea that he would be working at the Washington Post as an investigative reporter once he left the navy. But by extending his hand and making an effort to break the ice with a stranger, he changed the course of his life, American history and the lives of millions of people! He created his own luck.

Scarcity Principle

Walter

In his book *Awareness*, Anthony DeMello writes, "Our feelings of scarcity can inhibit the power of luck we are attempting to harness. It's so easy to fall into the trap of concentrating on what we don't have, rather than appreciating all that we do have and being grateful. It's impossible to be grateful and unhappy at the same time."

Remember back in high school when you had an enormous crush on someone but were afraid to ask for a date? You dreaded being turned down and having the whole school find out about it. If you were a typical teen with acne, any rejection made you feel like an undeserving schnook. Unbeknown to you, that pretty girl or handsome boy may have been sitting by the phone waiting for you to call. Your feeling of inadequacy caused a potentially wonderful experience to slip away.

Scarcity can force us into action. In school, did you ever procrastinate on a paper, only to pull an all-nighter and somehow manage to squeak out a decent grade? In this situation, a feeling of scarcity, and not having enough time, motivated us to take action and produced positive results.

When it comes to your money, scarcity is different. Thinking with a mentality of scarcity can be harmful to your financial health. Fear of not having enough money, even if your finances are stable, may rob you of the motivation to meet new people, leap into a new career, and create new experiences where luck has a chance to germinate.

"Golf is a game of luck. The more I practice,
the luckier I get."
Ben Hogan

Chapter Eight

Adjust Your Attitude, Build Your Cathedral

"It is our attitude toward events, not events themselves, which we can control. Nothing is by its own nature calamitous. Even death is terrible only if we fear it."
Epictetus

So much of what happens to us in life is the result of our attitude and determination. Two people can be working at identical jobs and have completely different perspectives.

There is a story about three masons laying bricks. Each is asked, "What are you doing?"

The first spits on the ground and says, "What the hell does it look like I'm doing? I'm laying bricks."

The second mason mops his brow and says, "I'm earning a living."

The third looks up to the skies and says, "I'm building a cathedral!"

Which of the three masons' attitudes sounds like yours? Do you see the cathedral or are you too busy laying bricks?

The third mason is doing a great job of enhancing his human capital. Aside from their perspective on their careers, the mason workers' story can also be used as a metaphor for the way we approach investing.

The first mason reminds us of people who worry at the first sign of market volatility. They interpret every minor news event as a precursor of a foreboding tomorrow. They check the value of their account daily. Like the mason laying bricks whose only vision was to finish his workday, these people are so engrossed with daily market fluctuations they don't embrace the importance of investing for their future.

The second mason has a somewhat better attitude. Although he may have thought he was achieving a goal by earning a living, he has trouble envisioning the future. The first two masons need to think about what life might be like after the cathedral is finished.

These investors typically lack the patience to weather serious market downturns like that of 2008. They may proclaim, "I'm in for the long term; I don't look at day to day fluctuations," but when volatility escalates and stock market declines, the "earning a living" investors have difficulty remaining patient and staying the course. They need to understand that saving and investing are as important as bricks are to the structure and support of the cathedral.

The third mason has an attitude that virtually ensures success, whether building a cathedral or a portfolio, despite the inevitable setbacks that occur in any endeavor. When it rains, he understands that eventually the downpour will end and the sun will shine again, continuing his work undeterred. His goal is to build a great cathedral, not to lay bricks or earn a living. When we experience a protracted period with poor market performance, such as the ten-year period from 2000 - 2010 where the U.S. stock market return was virtually zero, cathedral investors are able to avoid impulsive decisions or drastic changes to their portfolio.

Like the mason who lays bricks every day with the vision of the cathedral in mind, cathedral investors have a clear vision of what they are building for the future. They possess the attitude that no matter what obstacles may appear, they continue to move forward optimistically towards their goals.

After the cathedral is finished, there will always be the need for maintenance, such as checking the foundation for cracks and fissures. No building or monument is ever really "complete." Similarly, financial plans and investment portfolios must be continuously monitored for changes in asset allocation and adjustments to both short- and long-term goals.

The important thing is to stay focused on the long term. It's clear that the third mason in our story has his focus on the big picture. As a result, he is happier, more content and in control of his direction in life. Whether we focus our human capital on creating a career path or creating a portfolio of investable assets, in both cases we have the opportunity to achieve our goals.

Walter

Attitude makes such a dramatic difference in how we interpret the world around us. I know that every now and then I have been guilty of a bad attitude. It doesn't just affect the issue at hand. It affects my relationships, my stress level and everything surrounding me! I get caught up in the minutia and lose sight of the big picture. It's a personal goal of mine to try to avoid these episodes and maintain an attitude like the cathedral mason with whom I greatly resonate.

Once in a while, we need to put on a pair of Groucho Marx glasses, look in the mirror, laugh and ask, "Just how serious is this anyway?" We all suffer from an occasional hardening of the attitudes. Lighten up!

Attitude Adjustment

Our client Steve recently came in for a routine financial evaluation soon after his wife was admitted into a nursing home. Our usually cheerful and upbeat client appeared anxious and agitated. During our conversation he ranted about depleting his money and his concern about sufficient retirement income. Previously, Steve had always been confident about his finances, and we knew from our current analysis that he was on track to reach his goals. Upon further discussion we realized Steve was not reacting to a financial issue. He simply needed an attitude adjustment.

As a result of our lengthy discussion Steve realized that the feelings of loneliness and abandonment incurred by his wife's entering the nursing home were the basis of his anxiety and not a reaction to his investment portfolio.

In situations where we perceive our problems are generated by money issues, there may exist outside events over which we have no control, and which are the underlying causes of our anxiety. As advisors, we try to be informed about every aspect of a client's life that can affect his or her financial or emotional stability. But clients do not always share that information because they think it is irrelevant and are uncomfortable doing so.

A poor man lived with his wife and six children in a very small one-room house. They were always getting in each other's way and there was so little space they could hardly breathe!

Finally the man could stand it no more. He talked to his wife and asked her what to do. "Go see the rabbi," she told him, and after arguing a while, he went.

And so the poor man told the rabbi how miserable things were at home with him, his wife, and the six children all eating and living and sleeping in one room. The poor man told the rabbi, "We're even starting to yell and fight with each other. Life couldn't be worse."

The rabbi thought very deeply about the poor man's problem. Then he said, "Do exactly as I tell you and things will get better. Do you promise?"

"I promise," the poor man said.

The rabbi then asked the poor man a strange question. "Do you own any animals?"

"Yes," he said. "I have one cow, one goat, and some chickens."

"Good," the rabbi said. "When you get home, take all the animals into your house to live with you."

The poor man was astonished to hear this advice from the rabbi, but he had promised to do exactly what the rabbi said. So he went home and took all the farm animals into the tiny one-room house.

The next day the poor man ran back to see the rabbi. "What have you done to me, Rabbi?" he cried. "It's awful. I did what you told me and the animals are all over the house! Rabbi, help me!"

The rabbi listened and said calmly, "Now go home and take the chickens back outside."

The poor man did as the rabbi said, but hurried back again the next day. "The chickens are gone, but Rabbi, the goat!" he moaned. "The goat is smashing up all the furniture and eating everything in sight!"

The good rabbi said, "Go home and remove the goat and may God bless you."

So the poor man went home and took the goat outside. But he ran back again to see the rabbi, crying and wailing. "What a nightmare you have brought to my house, Rabbi! With the cow it's like living in a stable! Can human beings live with an animal like this?"

The rabbi said sweetly, "My friend, you are right. May God bless you. Go home now and take the cow out of your house." And the poor man went quickly home and took the cow out of the house.

The next day he came running back to the rabbi again. "O Rabbi," he said with a big smile on his face, "we have such a good life now. The animals are all out of the house. The house is so quiet and we've got room to spare! What a joy!"[30]

Writing in *Inc. Magazine*, Geoffrey James[31] has some fascinating thoughts on creating and maintaining a positive attitude. Among his suggestions are to "Adopt beliefs that frame events in a positive way. Spend at least 15 minutes every morning to read or listen to something inspirational or motivational. If you do this regularly, you'll have those thoughts and feelings ready when events don't go exactly the way you'd prefer."

"Your beliefs and rules about life and work determine how you interpret events and therefore your attitude. Decide to adopt 'strong' beliefs that create a good attitude. To use sales as an example:

Situation: The first sales call of the day goes poorly.
> *Weak*: A lousy first call means that I'm off my game and today will suck.
> *Strong*: Every sales call is different, so the next will probably be better.

Situation: A big sales win comes seemingly "out of nowhere."
> *Weak*: Even a blind pig finds an acorn once in a while.
> *Strong*: You never know when something wonderful will happen!"

James further exhorts readers to avoid the "angry or negative media...full of hateful people who make money by goading listeners to be paranoid, unhappy and frightened. The resulting flood of negativity doesn't just destroy your ability to maintain a positive attitude; it actively inserts you into a state of misery, pique and umbrage."

Attitude Adaptation

Another healthy way to strip away the annoyances that bug you is through meditation. It's a tool we frequently use to become centered, gain control, think clearly and remain focused on our ultimate goals.

> *"Suffering is due to our disconnection with the inner soul. Meditation is establishing that connection."*
> Amit Ray

The *Psychology Dictionary* defines meditation as "an exercise during which the individual enters an extended state of contemplation and reflection over a specific subject or their general existence, sometimes with a view to attain a differing state of consciousness."

Obviously, meditation can mean different things to different people. One thing most people have in common is misunderstanding how powerful it can be. In a mere few minutes, it can help you get "centered."

Whether conscious of it or not, everyone does it throughout their lives. How often have you come home after an exhausting day of work, plopped down on your favorite chair, closed your eyes and let out a giant sigh? Whether you know it or not, you have just meditated! Ever gazed into an aquarium for a few minutes and been mesmerized by the movements of the fish? That's also a form of meditation.

Taking it one step further, close your eyes for ten seconds and think of the most moving, beautiful scene you can remember. Recall the vision, sounds and smell of that idyllic scene. There you go; you have just meditated. You are practicing being mindful and living in the now.

"Meditation is the ultimate mobile device; you can use it anywhere, anytime, unobtrusively."
Sharon Salzberg

Chapter Nine

Ignoring the Noise

"If you don't read the newspaper, you're uninformed.
If you read the newspaper, you're misinformed."
Mark Twain

Walter

Some years ago, our family attended the Bonnaroo Music and Arts Festival in Manchester, Tennessee. This colorful event regularly draws crowds of over one hundred thousand people from all over the country.

When we attended, bands like Pearl Jam and Jack Johnson were headliners with smaller, lesser-known bands like Little Feat and Minus the Bear also appearing. The variety of musical styles emanating from the huge onstage speakers was transcended only by the diverse fashions and hairstyles of those in the audience.

Inside the Bonnaroo concert area was a series of tents, each capable of holding thousands of listeners. The tents were arranged in a large circle surrounding a central area consisting of shops and small restaurants where people would gather to decide which groups to hear. Different bands would be performing in different tents, many at the same time.

As I sat listening to the music, sipping a cold beverage in one of the restaurants, the sounds resonating from several different tents poured over me and collided in a tumultuous cacophony. It was difficult to hear one band or the other. It was only when I returned to one of the tents that I was able to distinguish the sound of a single band.

"If everything is amplified, we hear nothing."
Jon Stewart

It struck me how similar this experience was to the financial media noise we encounter each day. With 24/7 reporting and analysis of every micro movement of the markets and economy, it's easy for us to lose our long-term focus. This daily commentary on normal market fluctuations may cause us momentary fear and uncertainty.

We need an occasional reminder that all the momentary noise distracting us from our financial goals is transitory. Given the media's need to keep us tuned in, whatever perceived calamity is being reported today will be replaced by an equally alarming development tomorrow. Hence the frequently heard teaser prior to breaking for a commercial, "You won't believe what (fill in the blanks) so stayed tuned..."

Allie

It's not our intention to be overly harsh regarding the role of media. They have a job to do in reporting the news. But we have a job to do as well, and it includes helping our clients take the latest financial "breaking news" blast with a grain of salt.

Happily, most of the financial disasters and other mayhem they warn about never occur. But that doesn't stop some people from making emotionally driven investment decisions that jeopardize their long-term financial success.

Conversely, the media can play a critical role in perpetuating the "windfall myth" during periods when a market upsurge appears unending. Witness just two of the countless headlines supporting the dotcom bubble, right up until it all crumpled:

> "Dow 36,000? Why Stop There? Some Wall Street Pundits Say There's No Limit to How High it Can Go" - *National Post*, Oct. 2, 1999

> "Analysts Agree Market Has Only Witnessed Start of Internet fever; No End in Sight for Tech Craze" - *Morning Post*, March 26, 2000

But in late March of 2000, tech stocks suddenly plummeted. Once again, the media proved to be an unreliable source.

During the 2000 Super Bowl, 17 dotcom companies paid $44 million for ad spots, according to Bloomberg. At the 2001 Super Bowl, just one year after that bonanza, only three dotcom companies ran ads during the game.[32]

Look up newspaper headlines from years past and you will see that financial history tends to repeat itself. Consider this quote from the *Wall Street Journal*:

"A harsh air of gloom hung over the markets, sending investors fleeing stocks..."

"Welcome to Shouda, Wouda, Couda, the investment hindsight show."

That's not a quote from the financial crisis of 2008 but rather a description of the market decline of October 2002. There are numerous examples of the financial media predicting doom in response to swift market declines. In retrospect, it's often difficult to tell what year the headlines are from. Witness the following four covers from Time Magazine:

In just one decade, the magazine millions trusted for reliable information used its cover to predict impending doom in the financial markets four times!

Fortunately, the editors of Time were wrong...all four times. But their penchant for the dramatic illustrates how the media can frighten investors into making emotional decisions.

Walter

Your financial wellbeing is not contingent upon or associated with the day-to-day "noise" of the financial media but in the calmness of understanding how your finances are affected by your emotions. Only you have the power to harness your emotions, away from the cacophony of clashing sounds to the clarity of the music in the tent. Remember how the music set the nursing home patients free without confusion or impatience.

The media may adversely affect your financial perspective. Be aware of what is relevant news and what is hyperbole. Sources of news information serve their need to appeal to as broad an audience as possible. However, your financial situation is unique to you and your family. It may have nothing in common with the broad news reports pouring out of your television.

Chapter Ten

The "Aha!" Moment

"There's so much information on the internet. But people don't need more information; they need 'aha! moments,' they need awareness, they need things that actually shift and change them."
Jack Canfield

Once you are able to ignore the unwanted distractions of the media, uninformed friends and other external noise, your perspective begins to improve. Feelings of financial peace and comfort will replace the emotional turbulence and you will begin to see things differently. We describe this as having a *paradigm shift*.

Our clients who experience this often refer to it as the "Aha!" moment. It sometimes occurs suddenly, in response to something we discussed or an event the client recalls that provides a sudden burst of unusual clarity.

Famous people often cite an *Aha!* moment that changed their lives — and sometimes the lives of millions of others as well. Microsoft founder Bill Gates had a huge Aha! moment when he realized he would have to sell his product before he could even make it; Momofuko Ando, inventor of instant ramen, saw people lining up for soup on a cold day; Jan Koum, WhatsApp founder, could not afford to phone his father in the Ukraine; GoPro founder Nick Woodman was inspired to invent a sturdier adventure camera when he wanted to take pictures of himself surfing and there simply wasn't anything on the market to fulfill that need.[33]

Sometimes, the *Aha!* moment for our financial planning clients emerges more gradually. In either instance, there occurs a paradigm shift in how the client thinks about money. Invariably, it's an enlightening revelation.

Most of the financial problems people experience have less to do with investing their money than with divesting old habits and misguided ideas about money.

Many of these ideas have accumulated since early childhood, creating a financial personality that developed over the years and is driven more by emotions and behaviors than by money.

Walter
What memories come to mind when you think back to your childhood and the way your parents handled their finances? What were you taught? Did you learn important values about money? How did you treat money when you were a little kid? I used to think that having ten single dollar bills was a lot more money than just one ten dollar bill. Isn't that funny? The big wad of singles made me feel rich!

Our childhood experiences can indeed have a profound effect on how we deal with money in later years. When I first entered the investment business, an elderly woman came into the brokerage office and told us she had a large amount of money that she wanted to put into a guaranteed annuity. When we gave her the application to open the annuity, she handed us a dirty envelope with thousands of dollars stuffed into it. Twenty years earlier, she had buried the cash in her back yard to keep it safe. Talk about dirty money! This poor woman had earned no interest on her cash for two decades, all because it made her feel safe. When she was a child, her parents lost a lot of their savings in the Great Depression and she was apprehensive about investing in anything. The experience left her with a skewed mental accounting of how to treat money.

Much of the research for this book is based upon our experience meeting with clients over the years to discuss their financial goals. Most of these planning sessions revolved around family and lifestyle decisions, such as concerns for their children and when they would retire and what they would be able to do in retirement. At times, these discussions became highly emotional. Rarely, however, was the conversation about whether Microsoft was going to raise their dividend or if the Federal Reserve was going to raise interest rates. The meetings were almost always about the clients' fears and concerns about the future. They would talk about their disappointments or failures and how they could avoid repeating them.

Efficient Markets Dispel Media Hype

Prognostications and strategies emanating from the media have little to do with how the average investor's portfolio performs. From experience, we know that performance can be severely impacted by our behavior.

In addition to behavior it is also important to have an investment philosophy to follow. An investment philosophy can serve as the cornerstone for building a portfolio. One helpful thesis is called the Efficient Market Theory. It evolved from a dissertation in the 1960s by Eugene Fama, economic Nobel Laureate in ecomomics and the "father of modern finance."

The EMT hypothesis states that at any given time, the price of a security reflects all available information, and everyone has access to that information at virtually the same time. Therefore, there is no advantage in attempting to capitalize on breaking news, research, market timing, economic trends or other data.

Allie

Have you ever passed an Apple store in a mall, saw it jammed with customers including a class of second graders happily clicking away on iPads and thought, "should I buy some Apple stock?"

In that moment, you may have felt as though you just discovered something that others didn't realize: if children are learning on Apple products they will probably be Apple customers for life and that means Apple stock should soar in value for years to come?

That's the kind of thinking the Efficient Market Theory dispels. Since the markets are efficient and a security's current price reflects all information, attempts to outperform the market are essentially a game of chance rather than one of skill. So your Apple "insight" is no better or worse an idea than a bet on a horse running in the Kentucky Derby.

Suppose you read a newspaper report that Greece is being evicted from the European Union so you consider removing international stocks from your portfolio. Well, in reality, you are too late: the news is currently priced into the market and the stocks that you sold have probably already declined in value. Next, you read about a pharmaceutical firm being acquired by Merck. You jump online to buy the stock. Guess what? You missed it. The acquisition is already priced in. Tesla is deluged with 500,000 orders for its new $35,000 electric hybrid and you think the stock will be going up. Too late, you missed the boat...or rather the hybrid.

A related idea, sometimes called the "weak form efficient-market hypothesis," is the *random walk theory*, coined by Princeton economics professor Burton Malkiel in his 1973 book, *A Random Walk Down Wall Street*. It holds that market and securities prices are random and not influenced by past events, thereby making attempts to uncover patterns or take advantage of new information futile. The random walk theory also states that all methods of predicting stock prices are futile in the long term.

Another excerpt from Malkiel's bestseller: "A blindfolded monkey throwing darts at a newspaper's financial pages could select a portfolio that would do just as well as one carefully selected by experts."

Speaking at an *IMN Global Indexing and ETFs* conference some 40 years later, Rob Arnott, CEO of Research Affiliates, disagreed. "Malkeil was wrong. The monkeys have done a much better job than both the experts and the stock market!" The company randomly selected 100 portfolios containing 30 stocks from a 1,000 stock universe. They repeated this processes every year, from 1964 to 2010, and tracked the results. The process replicated 100 monkeys throwing darts at the stock pages each year. Amazingly, on average, 98 of the 100 monkey portfolios beat the 1,000 stock capitalization weighted stock universe each year![34]

If monkeys throwing darts can consistently do as well or better than the markets, how valuable is the opinion of the so-called experts you see on the financial news shows, or the hotshot brokers who call with a can't miss stock opportunity? For that matter, how can you expect your inherited or preconceived beliefs about money to serve you effectively when it comes to investing? You must find the courage to discard your destructive behaviors so you can change your perception about investing and money.

The bottom line is that you don't need any more tips or ideas about how to choose investments. Instead, if you pay attention to what is important in your life and finding personal fulfillment, the rest of your concerns will take care of themselves. It isn't getting the highest return on your investments that will bring you to your *Aha!* moment; it's pursuing and fulfilling your dreams. Further, the adversities you encounter along the way may contain the seeds for new and better things to come. Your biggest financial failures will present you with opportunities for future financial success. Cherish them!

We spoke earlier about the relationship between people's emotions and the mistakes they make with their money. Financial decision-making has little to do with money and everything to do with the emotions and behaviors you carry around inside yourself. These are the obstacles that interfere with you reaching your financial goals.

What If?

Suppose you were given the opportunity to be reborn as a blank sheet of paper with no fears, no worries, no preconceptions about money. What would change for you? How many of your current beliefs about money would you want to hang on to? What if the words failure and success were interchangeable and they were no longer used as barometers for measuring performance?

How about embracing adversity as an opportunity to learn and grow? What if your decisions about money were not based on media hype, the fear of making mistakes, what you learned as a child or what other people are doing? What if you were able to use your previous mistakes as tools to reinvent the way you think about money?

There are no all-encompassing answers to these questions. No financial analyst or chief marketing strategist has the answers. If you examine the track records of the so-called experts — if you can find them, that is — you will discover they are wrong as often as they are right.

The ultimate goal of your relationship with money should not be overnight riches or even to outperform the market. Investment returns are important, but they are not the only way to measure success. Your goal should be to find contentment, personal fulfillment and love in all aspects of life.

"What lies behind us and what lies before us are tiny matters compared to what lies within us."
Ralph Waldo Emerson

Your Financial Boat

Walter

When discussing these issues with new clients, we often bring up the analogy of a boat on a troubled sea. Since there are many factors to consider when piloting a boat — wind, ocean currents, tides and other boats in your vicinity — you must design a plan with a provision for safe shelter should something unexpected occur.

Our portfolios need to be constructed similarly to be able to withstand market fluctuations and volatility. The most important factor for our clients is to provide them with a safe haven for their money and the means to weather any unforeseen financial challenges.

"In the end, just three things matter: How well we have lived, how well we have loved, how well we have learned to let go."
Jack Kornfield

Chapter Eleven

Advisors Come In Different Shapes and Sizes

*"Finance is the art of passing money from
hand to hand until it finally disappears."*
Robert W. Sarnoff

What should you look for when choosing a financial advisor? Elegant offices and a laundry list of financial designations may be impressive and sometimes important but you would do better to find someone who shares the values and quality of life issues that are most important to you. Shared values and mutual respect create the bond from which a strong sense of trust arises!

After an initial exploratory meeting, you should feel an emotional connection with the advisor, and be confident that the advisor will devote his or her efforts towards keeping you financially secure. Beyond merely choosing investments for you, the advisor should engender a sense of trust. It's this trust that will allow the advisor to become an integral part of your entire financial life; including insurance, taxes and estate planning.

You want someone who makes you feel comfortable and confident, someone who communicates clearly and doesn't attempt to overwhelm you with financial jargon.

If you clearly articulate what's important to you, an advisor should be able to gather all relevant financial information. You need to provide the advisor with enough information to see if there is a good fit. Investments are like tools you use to build a house. You can't start a project until you have a complete plan, a blueprint of what you want your house to look like. Only then do we choose the tools to build it.

Choosing the right advisor takes some investigation and thought. You might ask for a referral from a friend who has had a satisfactory long-term relationship with his advisor and whose circumstances are similar to yours. Your accountant or attorney might be a good referral source as well. Do your parents have a financial advisor? This trusted family relationship already exists and you might resonate with someone at the firm closer to your own age who will identify with your lifestyle and financial goals. Obviously, you also want to ask any advisor you are considering for a few names of his or her current clients. Call them.

Advisor Types
Advisors employ a variety of styles and disciplines. Your responsibility is to choose one who fits your needs and your taste. Some advisors are affiliated with large brokerage firms; some work for insurance companies; some may be solo practitioners. Some charge a commission on every transaction; some charge a set fee based on the value of your account; some a combination of both. The various advisory descriptions can be confusing so let's dig a bit more deeply into the types of advisors you might encounter in your search.

Financial advisors are compensated in different ways, the most common being:

1. Hourly advice.
2. A fee based on a percentage of a client's assets under management.
3. A commission each time a product or investment is purchased.

As mentioned previously, some advisors combine these services while others are commissioned or fee only. While there are potential conflicts in all three compensation models, the one with the least is the fee-only model. These advisors are held to a high fiduciary standard. If you only want someone to conduct transactions, a commissioned advisor may be best. If you need occasional advice on financial matters, the hourly model may work best for you. If you want more comprehensive planning and investment advice, and a more personal long-term relationship, the fee-based model may be your best choice.

This type of advisory relationship is much like a partnership in that your interests and those of your advisor are aligned. Moreover, fee-only advisors have an incentive to closely monitor your investments as well as any changes in your plans or circumstances. Their compensation is directly linked to growing your assets. Advisors solely compensated by commission have inherent conflicts of interests when making investment recommendations.

Unless you are looking strictly for someone to offer brokerage services, recommend you look for an advisor with a CERTIFIED FINANCIAL PLANNER™ certification. This means the advisor is held to a fiduciary standard. The CFP® mark is reassurance that the advisor has an understanding of financial planning and has completed at least 30 hours of continuing education credits every two years to maintain the certification.

A good way of obtaining information about prospective advisors is through the ADV Part 2 A and B. All conflicts of interest, outside business activities and other important details about the advisory firm are listed in these compliance packets. By law, an advisor should provide you with these documents at one of your initial meetings.

A Genuine Interest

You want to feel as though your advisor is sincerely interested in learning about you, your family, interests, plans for the future, as well as your fears and financial biases. Like a good doctor, your advisor will ask pertinent questions, probing to understand your concerns and aspirations. He or she will want to know what money means to you, where you see yourself in ten or twenty years, assess where you are now and what you will need to retire comfortably.

Walter

If you encounter an advisor who does all the talking and doesn't ask questions, be careful. I recently went shopping for a new car, an experience akin to having oral surgery. The salesman at the local dealership was a talker. I mentioned I was thinking about a GMC Yukon but wasn't sure if it would meet my needs. Without asking what my needs might be, Mr. Loquacious launched into a 10-minute dissertation on the joys of owning a Yukon: popularity, warrantee, the variety of colors, equipment available, the special financing being offered, etc. He never responded to my concern about whether the vehicle was a good choice for me. He never inquired as to how I would be driving it, where I lived, the types of driving conditions I anticipated, and what was important to me in a vehicle. He just kept talking, electrified by the sound of his own voice.

Thirty minutes later, I walked out of the dealership without even negotiating a price. It was obvious he had no interest in my needs.

You want to find an advisor who will listen to your needs and respond, someone who instills confidence. You want an advisor who will take the time to listen and learn what your concerns are about money and your future. That's why God gave us two ears and one mouth.

Listening is so important in the client/advisor relationship yet I regularly meet with prospects that tell me the reason for leaving their current advisor is "he doesn't listen to me!"

Speaking of listening skills, I'm reminded of the story about poor old Fred, lying in his hospital bed, surrounded by hopeful friends and family, but apparently not going to make it. Suddenly, he motions frantically to his pastor for something to write on. The pastor hands him a pen and a piece of paper, and Fred uses his last bit of energy to scribble a note and then dies. The pastor thinks it best not to look at the note right away, so he places the note in his jacket pocket. As he is finishing his eulogy at Fred's funeral, the pastor realizes he's wearing the same jacket as when Fred died. "Fred handed me a note just before he died," he says, "I haven't looked at it, but knowing Fred, I'm sure there's a word of inspiration in it for us all…." Opening the note, he reads aloud, "Move! You're standing on my oxygen hose!"

See what I mean? Nobody listens! Good advisors are great listeners.

"There is music the moment you start listening. "
Marty Rubin

Little Tips

A good place to look for professional references is the CFP° Board or the National Association of Personal Financial Advisors (NAPFA).

Most advisors will offer a free consultation, which is an excellent way to get acquainted with the advisor's background, planning and investment philosophy. Don't expect most advisors to provide you with an investment performance history. Security Exchange Commission regulations are very strict regarding investment return advertisements. More frequently advisors will structure your investment portfolio based on your needs for income, growth and risk tolerance.

Upon starting a relationship with an advisor, you may receive a Client Service Agreement which explains the information and services the advisor or his company will provide for you. Among the services you should receive:

- A quarterly investment summary;
- Asset allocation guidelines that meet your risk tolerance and investment objectives;
- A description of all transactions;
- A fee payment schedule; and
- A description of your investment objectives.

Be wary of paying a hefty amount for an elaborate, leather-bound financial plan. There are so many variables that can occur to necessitate change: career change, unemployment, illness or injury, death of a spouse. Financial plans serve as a guideline, a reference to where you are and where you hope to go, but that's all. Regular meetings with your advisor to discuss changes and challenges are more helpful. The financial planning process is so dynamic that many financial plans become obsolete before many of the details come to fruition.

Get started with your advisor search as soon as possible. If you already have an advisor and something is nagging at you about the relationship, don't assume you are needlessly worrying. Get a second opinion.

The advisor you choose should construct an appropriately diversified investment portfolio that reflects your goals and legacy — which may not have the pizzazz of the flashy investment portfolios featured on the covers of financial magazines. Back in the late 1990s, just before the stock market bubble burst, financial publications were rife with cover stories touting "the best stocks to own for the next ten years" or "the best mutual funds to buy for the upcoming boom in technology." They made investing sound like a new form of entertainment, and it still goes on today.

Chapter Twelve

The Space Between the Notes

After spending countless hours listening to our clients talk about their finances, their families, their fears and their futures, Allie and I learned the importance of hearing not only what they say...but hearing what they don't say regarding money. As the classical music composer Gustav Mahler said, "It is not the notes being played, but it is the silence between the notes being played that contains what is best about the music." This insight can be the most revealing aspect of a financial planning session.

In our meetings, clients share their life goals, their experiences, and their challenges. Rather than the outlook for the stock market or what their retirement portfolio's rate of return was the previous quarter, we discuss important decisions affecting their financial future. Obviously, investment returns are important, but it's also important to focus on things like family, health, friendships and fun. Clients trust us to make it all possible by investing their money wisely. It's a responsibility we embrace.

One reason why we are able to relate to our clients on a more personal basis is that Allie and I have a different — and we believe healthier — outlook on money and life than many financial advisors. We feel it is far more important to discuss treating their families to a holiday vacation than talking about whether the market will go up or down next month. Markets and the economy are important aspects of financial planning, but if our clients are unable to enjoy their money, we don't feel as though we have succeeded as their advisor.

Walter

For a parent, nothing is more rewarding or endearing than to have your child follow in your professional footsteps. Having Allie decide to join my advisory practice was one of my life's happiest moments. Part of it was having the opportunity to share all I had learned over the years with her, But beyond that, I knew how bright and talented she was and the fact that she chose to share her gifts with me and my clients was a gratifying moment in my life.

It was apparent that Allie brought much more to the business relationship than her capabilities. She changed the way we were able to relate to our clients. Her presence opened the door to communicate more effectively with our existing clients, in particular with the children and grandchildren of our clients, i.e., the future generations. Being closer in age and sharing many of their interests, Allie can often relate to younger people better than I can. Our clients recognize Allie's competence and compassion. She has also solved a common problem faced by many advisors: a smooth advisor transition from one generation to the next.

Finally, Allie offers a fresh perspective on client issues. I sometimes feel like the coach of a professional football or basketball team. I'm in charge of helping people who have already achieved success, giving them guidance and leading them towards the goal of a championship. But regardless of how many victories or trophies we acquire, over time, my message may get a bit stale. The players may grow tired of hearing the same mantra, even if it is a valid one. Now along comes an assistant coach who shares my values but based on different life experiences, has a different twist on how to communicate to the players. That's a bonus Allie brings to our business as she interacts with our clients.

Of course, working with my daughter can have its challenges, too. One of them is recognizing the point at which my daughter is no longer "my little girl" but a woman with her own perspective and acquired knowledge.

A few years ago, Allie and I had just finished a meeting with an affluent client. I inadvertently told the client we had worked for an hour to prepare for the meeting. After the session, Allie reminded me that it took her, and the team, many hours to prepare. She expressed her disappointment in my failure to acknowledge the time that was dedicated in preparing for the meeting. As the discussion became more heated, I realized — as wisdom springs from old age — that I should let her articulate her concerns. As I listened, I thought back to her first birthday party when we played games, sang happy birthday, and celebrated with cake and ice cream. Amid all the excitement I yelled, "How big is Allie? How big is she?" On cue, she raised both arms to the ceiling as everyone yelled, "SO BIG!!!"

What an incredible flashback! It arrived uninvited during a time of heated emotion. As I listened to her speak, I was dazed, my mouth wide open with disbelief about the realization that she was no longer that little child and I was no longer that young father.

Our Unique Vision

As a firm, we try to differentiate ourselves from wealth managers who focus exclusively on investment strategy and performance. While these are important criteria, in most cases they are not the only factors in determining whether clients feel confident and positive about their future. Over the years, we've consistently delivered superior returns for our clients but that doesn't mean everybody is achieving their goals. Investment strategy and performance are important considerations, but what is more important is having a long-term vision of what you want your life to be, and how you want the future to unfold. It's that singular **vision** in the present moment that should guide you.

As planners, we are obliged to look ahead and plan for the future. We make financial assumptions to help our clients achieve their goals. We keep the potential consequences and the "what ifs" of the future in mind, but we make our best informed decisions in the present — combined with our *vision* for the future — resulting in the best outcome for our clients.

"Isn't it funny how day by day nothing changes, but when you look back, everything is different…"
Prince Caspian

It's human nature for people to believe things will continue as they have always been. But things will change at some point, we just don't know when. Sometimes it's necessary for us to read between the lines. Will the economy be the same five years from now? Will it change your financial situation? Will you be in the same career situation five years from now? Are you sure you will be making more money? Could your company downsize or be acquired and could your position be jeopardized? Will you still be living in the same house? Will you be living in the same state? For that matter, will you still be married or single?

Story from the Tao Te Ching:
One day while working out in the fields, the farmer's son fell and broke his leg. The villagers came to the farm and said, "My, that's a great misfortune. Your son has broken his leg: now he can't help you in the fields."

The farmer replied, "It is neither a fortune nor a misfortune."

A day later, the government troops came to the village looking for young men to conscript into the army. They had to leave the boy behind because his leg was broken. Again, the villagers came to the farm and said, "My, that's a great fortune."

The farmer replied, "It is neither a fortune nor a misfortune."

Then one day the farmer's only horse jumped the fence and ran away. The villagers came to the farm and said, "What a great misfortune that your horse has run away."

The farmer said, "It is neither a fortune nor a misfortune."

A few days later, the horse came back accompanied by a dozen wild horses. The villagers came and said, "It's a great fortune that your horse came back with twelve others."

Again the farmer replied, "It is neither a fortune nor a misfortune."

When things happen to us in life, we don't always know what they mean. The future is unknowable and mostly beyond our control, but it's neither a fortune nor a misfortune. The only control we have is control over the present moment. The present is what is happening in your life right now in real time. The present is where you have some control — not the past, which is over, and not the future with all of its uncertainty and variables. In the present moment you still may have experiences that are seemingly bad: you lose a job and feel devastated. But the loss of the job eventually turns into something positive: you find a new job in a relatively short period of time and are making twice as much money. In the present moment you may not know exactly what things mean, but you still maintain a vision of the most important things and people in your life. You have a vision of financial security. We believe if you hold these visions in mind in the present, they will manifest into what is meant to be.

Allie

My husband and I recently renovated our home. Before the architect and builder got involved, I had a vision of what I wanted the completed project to look like. I knew how I wanted the new kitchen to be laid out, what the countertops, cabinets and appliances would look like and where they should go. I didn't know the exact parameters or measurements, but in my mind, I had a clear picture of my family enjoying the new kitchen. I could see our extended family seated around the dining room table at Thanksgiving. When it was finally complete, the kitchen was not only what I had envisioned, it was better!

As planners, we keep in mind the clients' visions for themselves and what the end results should be. Their vision is the catalyst or seed for the dream to manifest.

We like to use the example of planting a peach pit in the ground. The pit contains parts of the past, present and future. It came from a tree in the past, but after being planted in the present, it will eventually manifest into a peach tree, given the proper growing conditions. Natural law then begins to unfold before our very eyes, whether we recognize it or not. Planning for the future is much the same. We look ahead and see the vision, whether a tree, a new kitchen or moving into the next creative phase in life.

Plans Don't Make Dreams Come True —
Dreams Make Plans Come True

Your vision is the core of your future and what moves you emotionally. Everything you do in the present should revolve around achieving that vision. If your vision is to retire and remain close to your children and grandchildren, what needs to be done now to ensure that happens? Maybe that means instead of moving to Florida after retirement, you plan to keep your current home and rent a smaller place in Florida for vacations. What will that take? How much do you need to save?

This is how visions become reality. You create the visions and then work backwards and discover ways to make it happen. **The future vision dictates the present steps,** not the other way around, as do so many financial plans. You have to first have the vision, then comes the plan. *Plans don't make dreams come true—dreams make plans come true.*

That's not to say you should be navigating blindly into the future. One reason many people fail to achieve financial success is that they made mistakes in the past and fear they will repeat the experience. One way to overcome past failures and fears about the future is to simply dream a little. Ask yourself, "What does money mean to me? What's important to me about money?" The money has to represent something other than itself. For too many people, it's all about accumulating money — but to what end? As their investment advisors, we understand the importance of identifying what money means to our clients, what they plan to do with their money and where they envision themselves 10, 20, 30 years or more down the road. It's that vision and the emotions associated with it that determine how we should manage their money.

Ideal and Acceptable Goals

Once we have a clear picture of the vision, we can create the plan to support it. We like to think of planning in terms of what is <u>ideal</u> and what is <u>acceptable</u>. For example, ideally, you might hope to retire at age 59, but if that proves impossible because you haven't saved enough, you would find it acceptable to work until age 65. This is an important concept.

You can apply this to virtually any goal. Let's say you're planning for the vacations you expect to take in the next year. You might say that ideally, you would like to allocate $20,000 for vacations: $5,000 on a trip to Jamaica, $5,000 for a two-week Alaskan cruise, and $10,000 for a family trip to Italy. However, if necessary, you would find it acceptable to forego all of those trips and only spend two weeks with the family at local resorts.

Thinking <u>ideal</u> and <u>acceptable</u> gives you more options from which to choose. The consideration is not whether or not you will go on a vacation but rather what type of vacation makes the most sense for the amount of money you apportion (assuming you do not have unlimited means). For example, *ideally*, you would like to leave all your assets and investments to your children, but you would *accept* spending some of your investments down in retirement and only leave them your primary residence.

In the present moment, each of us has an idea of the most important things and people in life. We believe if we hold your goals in the present moment, they will manifest like the peach pit in the ground. Without a vision, what are you working towards? Managing money and trying to grow it as much as possible? Without a clear picture, without goals, accumulating money is meaningless! What are you most passionate about? Listen to your heart. Hear the space between "your" notes.

Chapter Thirteen

Ways to Increase Your Dollars and Sense

*I'm not as concerned about the return on
my money as I am the return of my money.*
Will Rodgers

Bonds: The best form of income?

Most investors think of fixed income investments such as bonds,
CDs or annuities when they think of the best way to generate retirement
income. However, these are not the only vehicles that can provide cash
flow.

One of our clients called to say his bank was not providing him
enough interest for income. He wanted to know what bonds he should
buy to receive a specific dollar amount of income each month. We
explained to him that we have the ability to provide him a monthly
income from all of his investment sources (stocks *and* bonds). This
combination of dividends and capital gains is called 'Total Return'. It is
a better alternative than strictly bond income.

The following chart compares the income generated by two $10,000
portfolios from the years 1976 through 2014: one invested in dividend
stocks, the other in the Barclay's Aggregate Bond Index.

As you can see, investors buying a $10,000 bond paying 7% interest received $745 income in 1976 and just $253 in 2014 based on the ending value of $11,232. The same amount invested in the S&P 500 produced $451 of income in 1976, generated $4,452 of income in 2014 and the original $10,000 investment grew to $228,283 over the same time period!

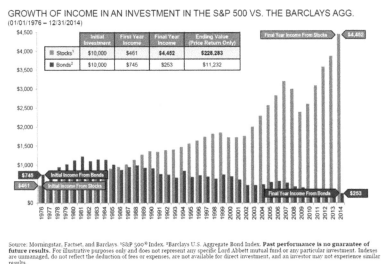

GROWTH OF INCOME IN AN INVESTMENT IN THE S&P 500 VS. THE BARCLAYS AGG.
(01/01/1976 – 12/31/2014)

	Initial Investment	First Year Income	Final Year Income	Ending Value (Price Return Only)
■ Stocks[1]	$10,000	$461	$4,452	$228,283
■ Bonds[2]	$10,000	$745	$253	$11,232

Source: Morningstar, Factset, and Barclays. [1]S&P 500® Index. [2]Barclays U.S. Aggregate Bond Index. **Past performance is no guarantee of future results.** For illustrative purposes only and does not represent any specific Lord Abbett mutual fund or any particular investment. Indexes are unmanaged, do not reflect the deduction of fees or expenses, are not available for direct investment, and an investor may not experience similar results.

Now skeptics might think, "Yes, but with bonds I have a very high likelihood of getting my money back at maturity." That is true, barring default, of course. But when held for the long term, stocks historically have delivered not only return *of* principal but also return *on* principal. For example:

- During any rolling 10-year period since 1970, S&P 500 returns — with dividends taken as income — equaled or exceeded the original investment 84% of the time. In addition to the dividend payout, on average, the principal would have doubled.
- During any rolling 15 or 20-year period, 100% of equity investors would not only have received their original investment, on average, it would have grown by more than three and five times, respectively.[35]

The purchasing power of bonds decreases over time while the cost of living continues to rise due to inflation. Stable, dividend paying blue chip companies historically do a better job of protecting purchasing power in retirement than bonds, outpacing inflation over the long term. Income from companies with a history of increasing dividends each year, such as Coca-Cola or Merck, can be very powerful. The money you receive today from your bond portfolio does not buy the same amount as it did a decade or two ago.

Bonds, CDs and annuities have a place in your portfolio, but we prefer a total return approach to income, combining bond interest, dividends and capital gains.

Timing the Market

Studies have shown it is futile to attempt to predict the future direction of interest rates or the stock market. You might think highly paid Wall Street financial analysts would have some insights into the future course of the market, but that's not the case. In an article from financial website, The Motley Fool, Morgan Housel notes, "In hindsight, everyone saw the financial crisis coming. The crazy lending, the high leverage, the soaring home prices. It all made so much sense. In reality, few did. Some saw troubles, or imbalances. But very, very few truly foresaw the magnitude of what would occur in 2008. And the surprise of 2008 wasn't ... a surprise. Wall Street analysts and economists have missed nearly every significant market turning point for as long as anyone can remember."[36]

According to Yale economist Robert Shiller, "In particular, if you look at the Great Depression of the 1930s, nobody forecasted that. Zero. Nobody. Now there were, of course, some guys who were saying the stock market is overpriced and it would come down, but if you look at what they said, did that mean a depression is coming? A decade long depression? That was never said. I have asked economic historians, give me a name of someone who predicted the depression, and it comes up zero."

A Dresdner Kleinwort study looked at Wall Street's predictions of interest rates over a 15-year period and compared them with what interest rates actually did, with the advantage of hindsight. It found an almost perfect lag. If interest rates fell, Wall Street would wait six months and then predict that interest rates were about to fall. When interest rates rose, Wall Street would wait six months and then declare that interest rates were about to rise. The report concluded that "Analysts are terribly good at telling us what has just happened but of little use in telling us what is going to happen in the future."[37]

A classic example of professionals being wrong was the overwhelming majority of "experts" who predicted Hillary Clinton would be elected president in 2016. A similar political event occurred in 1948 when the "experts" of the day concluded Tom Dewey would be the country's next president. Donald Trump and Harry Truman's victories proved them wrong.

It's almost impossible to accurately time the market. A 2010 Fidelity study analyzed the reactions of three different groups of investors to the market crash of 2008:

- Investors who reduced to 0% equity during Q4 2008 or Q1 2009 and subsequently remained out of equities until the completion of the study, March 31, 2010.
- Investors who reduced to 0% equity during Q4 2008 or Q1 2009 and moved back into the stock market at some point before March 31, 2010.
- Investors who stayed invested throughout, maintaining their current asset allocation.

The study revealed that investors who reduced their equities exposure to zero suffered a (-6.8%) return. Those who moved to 0% equity then jumped back into the market averaged a 6.1% return. Those who remained invested throughout the study period averaged a 21.8% return. The results reaffirm both the impossibility of timing the market as well as the destructive effect of investor behavior on investment performance.

Writing in the *Harvard Business Review*, author Jeff Stibel notes, "So how do we accurately predict where the markets are headed? The truth is, we can't. The future, like any complex problem, has far too many variables to be predicted. Quantitative models, historical models, even psychic models have all been tried — and have all failed.[38]

The best prediction machines we possess are our own brains. While a human brain cannot calculate a mathematical equation as quickly as most basic calculators, it can easily determine where a ball in mid-flight will land — without calculating its precise trajectory or velocity. Could you imagine trying to instantaneously calculate where a fly ball will land? Of course not, but I'll bet you could catch it.

Our brains are great at what they do because they make educated guesses — but that also makes us vulnerable to errors in judgment. Nowhere is this more pronounced than when we try to forecast the future.

The human brain is great at predictions but horrible at long-range forecasting. This is why we have no problem anticipating that a slithering snake might bite us and jump out of the way in a millisecond, yet we would have difficulty guessing where the snake will be the next time we go out into the yard.

"Far more money has been lost by investors preparing for corrections, or trying to anticipate corrections, than has been lost in corrections themselves."

Peter Lynch

Pension Faux Pas

The guaranteed income for life from defined benefit pension plans which so many Americans came to rely on hardly exists anymore. The emergence of the 401k has shifted responsibility for retirement planning from companies to individuals. The overwhelming majority of existing defined benefit pensions are now reserved for public sector employees — teachers, fireman, police officers and the like — who receive a monthly pension check when they retire. Whether a pensioned employee is retiring from a corporation or a public service position, it's critical to understand the payout options and their implications for the future.

Here are the typical payout options offered by defined benefit plans:

- Lump sum payout: A one-time distribution of the current value of the pension, with no future benefit available for either the retiree or beneficiary. This lump sum is considered a taxable distribution unless the amount is rolled into a 401k, 403b or traditional IRA.

- Life only annuity: Monthly payments that continue for the lifetime of the retiree exclusively (no payments to a beneficiary) and are treated as ordinary income for tax purposes.

- 50% Survivor annuity: Monthly payments that are reduced by half upon the death of the retiree and then paid out to the beneficiary for their lifetime, assuming the beneficiary outlives the employee. Typically, this option pays a smaller monthly amount than the life only annuity and is determined by the age of the beneficiary. The younger the beneficiary, the smaller the monthly payment.

- 100% Survivor annuity: Monthly payments that continue in full until the death of both the retiree and the beneficiary. Again, there is a reduced monthly benefit as compared to either the life only or the 50% survivor annuity payouts based on the age of the beneficiary.[39]

While the defined benefit pension provides employees with the assurance that they can rely on a specific amount of monthly retirement income, the potential for costly mistakes exists when choosing a payout option. Here are some generic options for pension benefit choices:

> Single Life: $5,000/month
> 50% Joint and Survivor: $4,000/month
> 100% Joint and Survivor: $1,414/month
> Lump Sum: $256,660

Single Life

John, a sergeant in the NYPD, was entitled to a $5,000 monthly pension when he retired. He chose the life only annuity in order to get the full $5,000 each month but passed away shortly after retiring. The benefit stopped when John died and unfortunately his wife was not eligible for continued monthly payments.

50% Joint and Survivor

Mike, a retiring firefighter for the FDNY, wanted to make sure his wife had income should anything happen to him so he chose the 50% survivor annuity. The couple received $4,000 a month until Mike died. After that, his wife continued to receive $2,000 a month until she passed. The benefits ended at her death. The three children and seven grandchildren were not entitled to receive the reminder of Mike's pension.

100% Joint and Survivor

Sara worked as a county clerk and was eligible for a pension. She chose the 100% Joint and Survivor option, allowing her and her spouse to receive $1,200 per month for as long as either of them remains alive. This option further reduces the current monthly benefit but will continue to pay out the same amount until the second spouse passes away.

Lump Sum Payout

Frank, a retired New York City sanitation worker, chose a lump sum distribution upon retirement. He rolled over $256,660 into an Individual Retirement Account (IRA). He opted for maximum flexibility to do what he wanted with the money. One of the benefits is that the balance of the lump sum payout is available to future generations. Hopefully the recipients can properly invest the money and generate a better monthly income than the annuity options provide, preserve liquidity, and leave any remainder to their beneficiaries.

Retirees who choose an annuity payout are guaranteed income for life without the responsibility of making investment decisions. The downside is being reliant on the financial stability of the employer and its ability to manage the pension funds effectively (most pensions have at least a portion of their payout insured by the Pension Benefit Guarantee Corporation). Another factor is whether the benefits have a cost of living adjustment to help offset the effects of inflation. Also, depending on the payout options, long-term income streams are not guaranteed to future generations.

Withdrawals

Money withdrawn from a pension plan prior to age 59.5 — or in some cases, age 55 — is subject to a 10% penalty in addition to the 20% federal withholding tax plus any state and local taxes due on the withdrawal. The penalty and taxes can be avoided by having your employer send the retirement funds directly to an IRA or, if you are changing jobs, to your new employer's pension or 401k plan, assuming it accepts rollovers. There is no penalty or withholding tax as long as the money is directly deposited with the new custodian.

Alternative Retirement Plans

Those not eligible to receive a pension have the opportunity to create a monthly pension check for retirement by using the money saved during their working years. If you have a 401(k), IRA or similar individual retirement savings account, your payout options are typically a one-time lump-sum payout or regular withdrawals from your savings. Some 401(k) plans also may offer an option to convert your savings into a lifetime monthly pension payment.

We encourage our clients to think about their entire individual investment portfolio, including individual investment accounts, bank accounts, joint investment accounts, as well as their retirement funds — as a potential source of monthly income. One of the major benefits in creating this personal income stream is that it does not stop when the recipient dies, as with most pension plans. The assets remain to pay out or to provide a lump sum or monthly checks for surviving spouses. When the surviving spouse dies, the money can continue to be paid out to children, grandchildren or future generations. This personal plan mimics what you would have received in retirement benefits from a typical corporate defined benefit plan, but with a lot more flexibility and longevity.

Gold

Is gold worth its weight in a portfolio? Gold does not earn money, pays no interest or dividends, and is worth only what another investor is willing to pay for it. Some people consider gold a doomsday investment; others see gold as an inflation hedge. A fellow we know stashed a few bars of gold in his basement, thinking that one day the economies and currencies of the world would collapse and gold would become the new currency. In such a scenario, who's to say what the new currency will be? Would it be gold? Who knows what gold would be worth, if anything at all?

Consider the performance of gold from 1971 through 2011. It wasn't a very good investment. Keep in mind that investors could not buy gold until 1975. The chart that follows documents the real growth of a dollar invested in gold versus equities over the forty-year period. Gold provided lower inflation-adjusted growth than other assets ($7.33 per dollar invested) and a lower average return: 4.9% per year versus 5.3% for the S&P 500, 5.0% for non-US stocks and 7.3% for US small cap stocks.

Real Growth of a Dollar
January 1971–December 2011

For illustrative purposes only. Sources for all figures: CRSP data provided by the Center for Research in Security Prices, University of Chicago; the S&P data are provided by Standard & Poor's Index Services Group; securities and commodities data provided by Bloomberg; MSCI data copyright 2012, all rights reserved. **Past performance is no guarantee of future results, and there is always the risk that an investor may lose money. The indices are not available for direct investment. Performance does not reflect the expenses associated with the management of an actual portfolio.**

Warren Buffet has some interesting thoughts on gold: "Today, the world's gold stock is about 170,000 metric tons. If it were all melded together, it would form a cube of about 68 feet per side and fit within a baseball infield. At $1,750 per ounce, it would be worth $9.6 trillion.

With the same amount of money, you could buy all U.S. cropland — 400 million acres with output of $200 billion annually — plus 16 Exxon Mobil's, the world's most profitable company, each one earning more than $40 billion annually, and still have about $1 trillion in cash"[40]

When you invest in gold, you are investing in a single commodity that does not provide income or growth. As Warren Buffet maintains, if you put it in the middle of a baseball field it just sits there. We think it's wiser for most people to invest in a portfolio of companies that create products and services, find cures for diseases and provide jobs; companies that give back to their investors a share of the profits in the form of dividends.

If you do insist on owning gold, instead of buying gold bullion, why not purchase some shares of the companies that sell picks, shovels or heavy equipment used to mine the gold? The prices of these stocks are tied to the value of gold. They provide dividends, and also may be good investments as you wait for the price of gold to increase.

> *"Gold is a commodity; over the long run, as we look back, it has not been a good investment. You can't look at the intrinsic value of gold as you can a business. Gold doesn't give you cash flow, and, at the end of the day, cash flow is what is important. Gold doesn't give you dividends."*
> Michael Lee-Chin

401(k): Employer Match = Free Money

If you could receive a 50% guaranteed return on your money with no risk, would you take it? Many companies that provide a 401(k) retirement plan also provide an incentive to invest by matching 50% of employee contributions. This means that for every dollar you contribute, the company contributes an additional $.50 into your account.

Congratulations! You just earned a 50% return on your money, guaranteed (subject to company vesting schedules) and you did not have to make any investment decisions. Companies typically match employee contributions up to a certain percentage of their salary, such as 6%. If, as an employee, you do not elect to defer at least 6% of your salary, you're not taking full advantage of this "free money" opportunity.

If you earn $50,000 a year and elect to defer 6% (or $3,000) of your salary into your 401(k), your company will match $1,500 into your account, leaving you with a total of $4500 at the end of the year, in addition to any investment gains or losses. Instead of having $3000 to invest, grow and compound, you now have $4500. This can make a huge difference as you save for retirement.

Along with the opportunity for free money, starting to save as early as possible is just as important. The following chart illustrates this point:

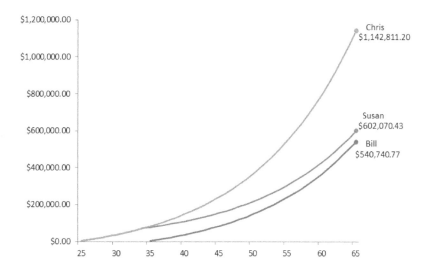

The above illustration is a hypothetical example and does not reflect actual investing in any client accounts. It assumes the investments earn an annualized rate of return of 7% per year.

Susan invests $5,000 annually between the ages of 25 and 35. Her contributions over 10 years total $50,000.

Bill invests $5,000 annually between the ages of 35 and 65. His contributions over 30 years total $150,000.

Chris invests $5,000 annually between the ages of 25 and 65. His contributions over 40 years total $200,000.

It's obvious Chris's retirement account at age 65 should far exceed those of Susan and Bill. He contributed for the longest period of time, 40 years, and his contributions were greater.

Susan's retirement balance perfectly exemplifies the power of compounding, proving the benefits of investing at an earlier age than Bill. She contributed only $50,000 of her own capital and stopped contributing into her account the year Bill began! Susan's retirement portfolio was greater than Bill's at age 65.

> *Compound interest is the eighth Wonder of the World. He, who understands it, earns it...he who doesn't...pays it.*
> Albert Einstein

Why Equities?

We invest in the common stock of innovative companies to provide the wealth we need for retirement. In addition to financial gain, we have also borne the fruits of their innovation through the years, advancements that have been the foundation of the great technological developments we enjoy today. Breakthroughs in medicine, pharmaceuticals, transportation, electronics, communications, natural resource exploration, robotics and other technologies have produced breathtaking improvements in the quality of our lives. Our children and grandchildren will hopefully have the ability to see cancer eradicated. From the miniaturization of medical instruments and noninvasive surgery to discovering diseases earlier and treating patients better, innovation has touched us all in some way.

Did you know that you have an impact on these innovations as well? You have the opportunity to invest in companies that are both profitable and dedicated to creating breakthroughs to help humanity — not merely to extend life but also to improve the quality of life.

*"The real key to making money in stocks is not
to get scared out of them."*
Peter Lynch

These companies comprise the great market of stocks that have the potential to help society and to improve our lives. As American and international companies prosper and grow, their research and development provide newer and even greater opportunities. Even though stocks are volatile, the benefits of investing in companies whose products have a major impact on the lives of people around the world should far outweigh daily fluctuations in the stock market.

Should You Pay Off Your Mortgage?

Our friend Joe was determined to pay down his mortgage because he felt strongly about living debt free. He was allocating so much of his income towards his mortgage that he was unable to save for his family and his retirement. We asked Joe where his income was going to come from after he stopped working. He needed more income per month than his social security check. The answer was obvious. By paying off his house, he severely limited the amount of income he would have available for retirement.

Is aggressively paying off your mortgage always the right financial decision? We do not necessarily advise our clients to do so. Your mortgage is like a bill you pay for your home, a bill you pay to yourself. As you pay down what you owe, you create equity while simultaneously investing in more real estate. You must consider if paying off your mortgage is as important as contributing monthly to an investable savings account (such as a 401(k)). For us, it is not financially prudent to regard your home as your principle investment. Pouring your discretionary income into your primary residence by paying off your mortgage may not always turn out to be a good long term strategy.

Think of your mortgage as just another bill that you need to pay as you figure out your cash flow for the month. The tax deduction is certainly a worthwhile advantage. If you are in a 40% tax bracket, and the interest rate on your mortgage is 5%, it's only costing you 3% out of pocket.

One trick that will help cut down on the amount of interest owed on your home is to split the monthly amount into bi-weekly payments. Instead of paying $3,000 a month, pay $1,500 every two weeks. You end up making one extra mortgage payment each year which can result in paying off your mortgage years faster, while still leaving some wiggle room for other savings opportunities.

These financial pointers — and indeed this book — represent our best ideas to help you become a knowledgeable, savvy investor. Despite what you may hear from some members of the financial community or the media, successful investing is not about discovering some cryptic financial secret or investment strategy. It's about unlocking the door to *The Millionaire Within!*

"Worrying is like paying on a debt that may never come due."
Will Rogers

Chapter Fourteen

What She Tackles She Conquers:
Women on the Move

The evolution of women over the past century has been amazing. Only in the last hundred years were women given the right to vote. A mere sixty years ago women were typically stay at home mothers, and it wasn't until the 1970's that women were given equal opportunity for federal funding, with the passage of Title IX. Today's women enjoy an unprecedented level of independence as well as an extraordinary amount of personal and professional opportunities!

Allie

I think of women as constantly being in a state of transition. Whether it is a societal shift as to how we are perceived, or the evolution of gender roles, a woman's identity is frequently re-defined. Aside from societal advancement, women are continually redefining their roles throughout their lives. No matter what stage of life, whether furthering a career, raising a family, dissolving a union, approaching retirement or surviving the death of a spouse, a woman is almost *always* in transition.

Feminism isn't about making women strong.
Women are already strong. It's about changing
the way the world perceives that strength.
G.D. Anderson

The stereotype of the financially passive woman of the past has been replaced by today's empowered woman, more than capable of juggling career, family and whatever else she chooses to have — or not have — in her life. It's an important distinction because whether single or married, with or without children, women today are no longer willing to allow themselves to be subjected to financial uncertainty. If married, they usually want to be equal financial partners, independent of their spouse's income. If single, they must be fully engaged in their financial futures.

Walter

Women's status in the world of business has increased dramatically over the past two decades. In 1998, there were only two women heading up Fortune 500 companies. By 2014, that number had increased to 24. Today there are 51 women serving as CEOs of Fortune 1000 companies.[41] While the number of top women executives is not on a par with men, women continue to make huge strides in their careers, in the boardroom and elsewhere.

Allie

A study published by the American Sociological Association revealed that approximately 51% of Millennial women either earn as much as their husbands or are the primary breadwinners. According to Pew Research, today's young women are starting their careers better educated than their male counterparts.

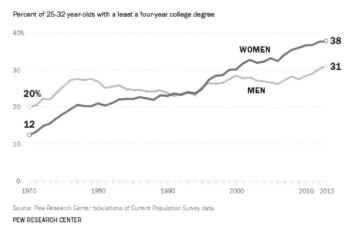

Percent of 25-32 year-olds with a least a four-year college degree

Source: Pew Research Center tabulations of Current Population Survey data.
PEW RESEARCH CENTER

Pew also reports that as well as being more educated than ever, there is less traditional pressure for women to conform to the institution of marriage, to raise a family or to seek some role that is simply stereotypical. While 48% of Baby Boomers (over age 50) and 36% of Generation X (ages 37 – 50) married between the ages of 18 and 32, only 26% of Millennials (under age 37) married at the same age.

Walter

Despite graduating with more college degrees than men and having more power and earning potential than ever before, a survey conducted by Dailyworth.com found that while 90% of women identify themselves as the chief bill-payers and shoppers for the household, 60% of them thought their investing and planning skills were below average.

According to the Employee Benefit Research Institute, roughly the same number of full-time employed men and women participate in retirement plans. However, men contribute far more to those plans, with a median account balance of $31,388 compared with women's $20,877. Despite the reduction in the gender pay gap, the female financial paradox has continued unabated.

The disparity in retirement savings, combined with low levels of confidence in personal wealth management, often leads to a disconnect between earning money and building wealth and financial security. Experts have identified key factors underlying the paradox: women tend to be insecure about the subject of money; they focus on scrimping instead of investing; and they're not always adept at translating abstract figures into concrete goals.[42]

In our experience, most men do not understand how women are wired. Women think about money differently. Once they acquire money they make different decisions with it than men do because they interpret things differently. Because of this, there is potential for women to be more successful investors than men over time. Women tend not to let their emotions or ego get in the way. They are more likely to seek professional advice about money and investing. Unlike men, who tend to gravitate to the latest hot stock or flashy investment, women are more likely to be cautious and analytical about their investments.

Allie

My friend Molly became a client before getting married. She was in her thirties, had built a unique reputation throughout the fashion industry and her services were in high demand. Molly's income had recently increased in her new position, but she had no savings or emergency fund to fall back on. She was single, enjoyed spending money, and lived in a beautiful apartment in Manhattan.

As we began working together, she regretted waiting 15 years to save for her future. I instilled in her the importance of creating wealth for herself. We implemented a savings plan. As Molly became more financially savvy, she was able to maintain her lifestyle while still being able to save into her 401k and taxable savings accounts. Today, she is in more control of her money. Every conversation with her is an educational experience. In addition to coaching her about finances and investing, I also provide a sounding board for her potential career opportunities.

In the relatively short time we have worked together, Molly has fully embraced the feeling of empowerment she achieved by becoming more knowledgeable about her finances. She is now married. Her husband also has a thriving career and they both make financial decisions together. She loves her family and her career and she contributes significantly to their household income. More than anything, she appreciates the financial freedom she has created for herself.

In helping women like Molly and others transition through different stages of their career and family, it's apparent to us that they have become more independent and more in control of their lives. Many, however, need to be more cognizant of their finances and the consequences of the financial decisions they make — or don't make. Women have overcome job security and advancement issues but they still face challenges overcoming the financial obstacles that stand between them and their personal and career goals.

Interviews with Women

Allie

Independent women — whether single, divorced or widowed — represent a large portion of our client base. We began by serving a few women we knew in the community. They introduced us to their circle of friends and in a short period of time, our company evolved as a specialist for women and their money. Our company decided to conduct a survey of their thoughts about money, finances, working with a financial advisor and other related issues. The research proved to be more daunting than we thought. We expected the roughly 30 interviews might take 10-15 minutes each to ask a dozen questions, but they lasted much longer. All of the women we interviewed showed a genuine interest in talking about their money and finances.

Broken down by age groups, here is a synopsis of what we learned:

<u>Ages 20-40</u>

The most important factors were family, advancing careers, knowing where money is going, and finding the balance between careers and raising a family. They admitted needing help and many turned to their parents for financial assistance and advice.

Their fears included not having enough money, career security, retirement, losing family members or their spouse dying unexpectedly.

Regrets included not spending enough time with a family member who passed away, not pursuing their passion in some form, not starting to save sooner, and ignoring their finances.

<u>Ages 40-60</u>

These women expressed a huge emphasis on finding the balance between career and raising a family, organizing their finances and staying on track for retirement.

Their fears included not having enough money, being homeless, coming to the end of life and not having made a meaningful contribution.

They regretted not managing money better, relying too heavily on their husbands and not being more actively involved in the finances.

<u>60s and older</u>

Most important was family, health, having enough money for retirement, getting enough sleep and finding a new challenge in retirement.

Their greatest fears were their children's financial stability, passing away without having an impact or leaving a legacy, feeling unfulfilled, loneliness, and growing old alone.

They regretted not spending enough time doing what they enjoyed and not maintaining a better work/life balance.

Alfred Adler: Push-Pull Theory

Alfred Adler was a popular American educator and lecturer. He founded the neo-Freudian school of psychoanalysis. He balanced the equally important needs for optimal individual development and social responsibility.[43]

Adler identified the dichotomy between being *pushed* through life by circumstances and events; as opposed to being *pulled* through life by our passions and desires. When we are being pulled towards a goal, we feel a sense of control and empowerment. Conversely, when we are forced into uncertain pathways — such as a woman experiencing divorce or the death of a spouse — we are pushed into circumstances that make us feel trapped. When this happens to men *or* women, there is a sense of disempowerment and loss of control.

If you feel like you are *pushed* into an unfulfilling job because you need to earn a living, you may feel uncomfortable or dissatisfied. Conversely, if you are *pulled* to a career where you feel happy and accomplished, you will be more at peace.

Death and Divorce

While working with women over the years, we have come to realize that many of them who undergo a transition due to a divorce or the death of a spouse become inadvertent victims.

"And when you're alone, there's a very good chance you'll meet things that scare you right out of your pants. There are some, down the road between hither and yon, that can scare you so much you won't want to go on."

Dr. Seuss

These women often feel alone and believe they have insurmountable financial challenges. Many are transported into an unfamiliar environment. We try to alleviate their insecurities and fear of the future. We remind them they have the control and power to gain a clearer understanding of what is going on in their lives.

According to a study by economists Claudia Olivetti of Boston College and Dana Rotz of Mathematica Policy Research, the later in life a woman divorces, the more likely she is to be working full time. Using survey data on almost 56,000 women, they found that women who divorced in their 50s were about 10% more likely to be working full time from ages 50 to 74, compared with women who divorced before age 30.[44] Women tend to be more financially challenged than men after a late-in-life divorce. The poverty rate for men who divorced after age 50 is 11% compared to 27% of women.

The dynamics are shifting for women. In the past, Baby Boomer women tended to be less involved in financial decisions than their Millennial and Gen X counterparts. Today, women are becoming more engaged and more invested than ever before. 80% of women are currently involved in managing household finances.[45] Today more women have the opportunity to be involved in financial decisions, careers, literally every facet of their lives. The cultural dynamic has shifted. Millennials are able to capitalize on this newfound opportunity. Many women of previous generations overcame decades of ingrained bias and prejudice, yet today they have a greater ability to take control than they ever have in the past. Women of all ages have the tools needed to engineer a new future for themselves.

"Women, like men, should try to do the impossible. And when they fail, their failure should be a challenge to others."

Amelia Earhart

Elizabeth is a new client. She is in her late 50s and lives with her 25-year-old son in a small apartment. After a lengthy five-year divorce proceeding she finally received a settlement. Her ex-husband is the CEO of a major non-profit organization with a salary at least ten times greater than hers. Their marriage crumbled after he met a much younger woman at work.

During our initial meetings, we always ask our clients about their best and worst financial decision. In Elizabeth's case, her worst financial decision was not being involved in family financial decisions. During the divorce proceedings her lawyer discovered hidden checking accounts and pockets of money he stashed away in certain investments and institutions. She regrets not being more knowledgeable of her finances during her marriage as she may have had more leverage during her divorce proceedings.

Elizabeth's best financial decision? Becoming more educated in personal finance. Elizabeth's settlement was not sufficient for her and her son to live comfortably. Though Elizabeth feels she has to "start over," she is gaining confidence and taking the best steps to move forward in her life.

Financial independence for women in the 21st century is hugely important because traditional family "roles" have shifted. People are living together, without marriage. Single parent households are more prevalent today than ever before. Women are taking a stronghold in the workplace *and* within their families. Elizabeth does not view her situation as unfortunate. She considers her divorce an opportunity to create a much different life for herself: a life of strength, purpose, and financial clarity. Her path may not be what she envisioned when she got married many years ago, yet she is happier today than ever before.

When we have meetings where one partner has been making all the financial decisions in the relationship, we make the extra effort to include the other partner in our discussion. Regardless of their ages, whether they are working or retired, it's never too late to be mutually engaged.

We spoke in a previous chapter about people having an "Aha!" moment. We want the women who are our clients to experience that "Aha!" in recognizing their new sense of empowerment and how it can help create a more fulfilling future. This is true whether they are members of the Baby Boomer, Millennial or Generation X. There's a possibility women may be living independently at some point in their lives and may need someone — a trusted advisor or friend — to help guide them in the right direction. Most friends and family members are well-intentioned, but may not offer purposeful advice, especially financial advice.

Suggestions for Maneuvering Independently through Life's Transitions:

- **Avoid making major decisions during your grieving period:** whether to remain in your current home, relocating, investing money from a divorce settlement or insurance proceeds. Your emotions may cause you to make unwise decisions.

- **Get professional help**: If you are uncertain about any money issues, such as monthly income needs, cash flow, debts and the like, talk to an expert. This is no time for advice from friends or family members who are unlikely to be qualified to offer the financial advice you need.

- **Find a properly qualified attorney to settle your spouse's estate:** This may coincide with your financial issues, depending on how your spouse's assets were titled, especially in the case of second marriages. Children from the first marriage may object to financial choices made when their parents remarry. If divorcing, be mindful of attorney fees and attachment to assets. The longer the divorce drags on, the more expensive it becomes. You might consider mediation as an alternative.

- **Understand your options:** Dorothy, who was recently widowed, wanted to gift her husband's death proceeds to her grandchildren (ages 11-22) in the amounts of $14,000 annually — the maximum allowable annual gift. While the amount is allowable, what is an 11-year-old going to do with that amount of money? Is there an account set up for him? Is Dorothy's daughter capable of managing the money for the grandchild in the interim? Sometimes, it's not the amount of money we lavish on our children or grandchildren, it's what we do with them — family outings, vacations, events — that they will remember.

- **Don't hesitate to exercise control during your marriage:** Too often, one spouse handles all the finances and the other spouse is left uninformed and is rendered helpless when death or divorce occurs. It's OK to ask a lot of questions, shop around for professionals you feel you can trust, and get recommendations from friends.

Katharine Graham and Warren Buffett

When women experience the loss of a spouse, or another major transition in their lives, they may find themselves paralyzed by lack of experience in managing money, financial affairs, or even the day-to-day activities involved in running the household. We spoke with our friend, Weston Wellington, from Dimensional Fund advisors. He related to us a wonderful story about Katharine Graham and Warren Buffett that illustrates how women underestimate their abilities to be truly successful.

Katharine Graham was the wife of Philip Graham, co-owner and publisher of The Washington Post. Philip committed suicide in 1963 and Katharine was left to oversee the entire Washington Post operation. Her expertise in journalism was *very* limited, yet she suddenly found herself running one of the most prominent newspaper publications in the country. Because of her lack of experience, Katharine was often looked down upon by her male colleagues. Warren Buffett befriended Katharine after he became a major shareholder of The Washington Post. He provided her with his business acumen and helped her discover she already possessed the characteristics of leadership and good judgment that would help her become a successful businesswoman. Mr. Buffett convinced her that a journalism degree was unnecessary. Katharine had a lot more talent and ability in running the business than she realized. Under Katharine's leadership, she took bold initiative to publish government documents regarding the Vietnam War and the Nixon presidency against her lawyers' advice, invoking freedom of the press. Katharine was one the first women to lead a prominent American company and became a major advocate for women in the workforce[6].

Allie

Age, background and experience do not matter. Financial freedom and independence are the **greatest** *motivating factors for women and their money.*

Allie Vanaski

We have a recently engaged family friend named Amy. She graduated medical school last year and is now working as a medical resident in a promising surgical field. Amy is not yet earning a large income but her fiancé works for a technology firm and is well paid. While they are not clients, we spoke casually about their finances and earnings as a "power couple." Amy mentioned she needed to work on her prenuptial agreement. We didn't get into the specifics of the agreement, but Amy knew her future earnings power as a surgeon would constitute a large portion of the household income. Regardless of her specific intentions, it was refreshing to hear a young woman place such importance on her financial independence and take such strong control of her finances in a relationship. It's yet another reminder that women's roles in relationships are changing. Women earn — or plan on earning — significant incomes and don't want to depend on anyone else for financial security. They want to protect their money and be financially independent.

An Empowering Paradigm Shift

Allie

Today's women are empowered like no previous generation of women. Millennial and Gen X women are different from any generation that precedes us. We are graduating in record numbers from top colleges. As an economically, socially and politically powerful group, we enjoy newfound independence and unprecedented freedom to choose our careers and lifestyles. Many of us have our own money and priorities for managing it. We have greater control over our lives than our predecessors and we are no longer dependent upon men for money, security or opportunities.

This transformation from past generations is obvious. Women today have been liberated from the restraints of choosing between motherhood and career. Millions of women successfully balance the two. Women who choose to stay home and raise a family are no longer isolated, thanks to internet access and continued technological innovations. The confluence of better educations, greater freedom, and expanded career and lifestyle opportunities has combined to change the economic landscape for women. The role of the modern woman continues to evolve, steadily growing stronger and providing greater independence. It's a seismic societal shift and today's women are enthusiastically embracing the transformation. They share financial decisions with their husbands, whether or not they bring in an income. They are an integral part of the shared family relationship.

Walter

I recently went to daycare with Allie to pick up the grandchildren, I watched as she went about getting her two children safely tucked into her car. Her two-year old resisted being put into his car seat and her five-month old was crying and wanted her pacifier. I thought about how challenging it must be to balance motherhood and career. A flashback took me to the time when she was three years old. I opened the car door and held her hand as she climbed into her car seat. I think of the years that have passed and her role today as a wife and a mother. How she wakes in the middle of the night to feed and nurse her baby, then gets up in the morning to pack them both in the car to drive to day care, and then to work. After work, she picks them up and drives 45 minutes to arrive home at six o'clock, feeds them and puts them to bed. She prepares dinner for her and her husband and falls asleep only to repeat the process again the next day.

This snapshot of my daughter within her family is only a part of her day-to-day responsibilities. Allie is an integral part of our organization. During the typical work day, she juggles phone calls, attends meetings, travels to see clients and responds to operational and client requests all day long, sometimes interrupted by daycare issues, forcing an unintended change in her schedule. At the end of a long workday, she has this amazing ability to transition into a wonderfully caring mom and wife...and her day is not yet over.

Besides her busy and blossoming career as a financial advisor, she is writing this book and talking to clients all day. It continually amazes me how she is able to juggle all her responsibilities and still do everything so well.

I recall a first meeting with a new client, a successful single woman. Her appointment was with me but as soon as I introduced her to Allie, I may as well have left because the two of them hit it off immediately. I hardly spoke a word during the meeting as she and Allie conversed about everything from her job to her choice of cosmetics. At the end of the session, I recall getting up to escort her to the door, but she and Allie were already on their way out, leaving arm-in-arm, and I was left standing there. The two continued their conversation and have since built a strong advisor-client relationship, as well as a great friendship. It was a dose of humility for me but an important lesson as well. Today's conscientious women call for a different kind of advisory relationship, one of caring, mutual respect, and the confidence that what they both tackle, they conquer.

Women are truly superheroes.

It was never a dress.

Chapter Fifteen

Unleashing the Millionaire Within

"It's difficult to plan for what MIGHT happen.
We can only plan from what IS happening."
Walter Wisniewski

We believe the potential to be a millionaire resides within virtually everyone. By millionaire, we mean not just financial wealth but personal fulfillment as well.

We understand the challenges inherent with our money in relation to our behaviors and emotions. Our biases, childhood impressions and attitudes about money sometimes threaten our ability to make sound investment decisions. Noise from the media, the financial community and others impede us from finding the truth. Our senses and instincts betray us; our perceptions distort reality.

Making informed financial decisions is less about money than it is about our behaviors, beliefs and perceptions. We learned these things in previous chapters.

How do you overcome the obstacles that prevent you from unlocking that millionaire and achieving financial security? How do you reach inside to find the "Aha!" moment that leads to contentment and a well-balanced life?

Hopefully, this chapter will get you thinking about some of the transformations you can make in your own life, so you can begin to unleash the millionaire within.

Perception Deception

"It isn't what you don't know that gets you in trouble.
It's what you know for sure that just isn't so."
Mark Twain

This deceptively simple quote contains a profound truth. It's relatively easy for us to fall prey to misperceptions. An isolated financial setback or continued exposure to negative financial news can skew our perception of reality. Whether our perceptions are about our finances, family, friendships or career, we must be mindful of the many ways we can interpret conversations and events in our lives. In his insightful book, Quiet Leadership, David Rock notes, "It is our interpretations of the facts, our decisions our brain makes of inputs around us, that determine how we perceive reality."

How often have you experienced situations where you perceive things one way and, after getting more information, realize you may have been interpreting those things incorrectly?

Recognizing Value

Diamonds are an interesting metaphor for the state of the economy and the financial markets. As they appear when first unearthed in their natural state —these raw chunks of carbon appear opaque, like a lump of molten glass, their beauty and value obscured. Just as the South African farmer who sold his farm to look elsewhere in pursuit of diamonds, if you didn't know what a diamond in the rough looks like, you could literally stumble over one and not recognize it. Similarly, during any stock market downturn, it may be difficult to discern how/if/when an investment portfolio may recover. The gloomy environment painted by the media and pundits makes things appear considerably bleak. But like hidden diamonds below the earth's surface, the murky atmosphere of an economic malaise may be hiding financial opportunities from view. When we look closer, we discover that hidden within the negative news is an enormous opportunity to create wealth.

The metaphor of the hidden value in an uncut diamond can serve to change our *perception* from one of scarcity and fear to one of opportunity and change.

Staying in the Moment

Erroneous perceptions are one reason people do not recognize the millionaire within themselves. Failure to stay in the present moment can have a similar effect.

Walter

Do you know anyone who seems unable to enjoy what is happening right now, someone who is constantly talking about what will happen next? I had a fishing buddy like that. He would be so excited about our next excursion that he could hardly talk about anything else...until we got out on the boat and dropped our lines into the water. Once there, despite the beauty all around us, the serenity of the waves lapping gently against the side of the boat, and the companionship of a close friend, he immediately began talking about what we would be doing once we got off the boat. He was simply incapable of savoring the moment, of "smelling the roses," as they say.

There are so many variables affecting future financial decisions. The past is over and out of your control, and it's impossible to know the future with certainty. It's only in the *present* that rational decisions are possible because you have clearly defined choices immediately available. As a minister once told me, "If you want to give God a good laugh, tell him about your plans for the future."

It's difficult to plan for what might happen. We can only plan from what IS happening.

If you stay in the present moment, you can make directional changes that could have a positive effect on a situation's outcome. It's in the present where you can map out a new course, and even the smallest changes can have a huge impact (perhaps liberating your millionaire within) even though you may not realize it at the time.

Allie

There is a resort island off the coast of Georgia called Sea Island. Years ago, there were many activities at the local resorts including Land Sailing. These boats are similar to sail boats in the water, the only difference is they have wheels and can be propelled by the wind on the hard, sandy beaches. Interestingly, as you are "driving" along the shore it is possible that another land sailboat may approach from the opposite direction. As you pass each other, you realize there is only one wind blowing and the boats are going in opposite directions. How is that possible? Centuries ago, sailors learned how to chart a course *into* the wind, a process called "tacking".

In our daily lives, we have winds blowing on us all the time. They could be winds of opportunity or winds of adversity. Yet, it is not the winds blowing on us that determine our direction in life but rather how we navigate our course in the present moment. In other words, **it is not the gale but the set of our sail that determines our course in life.**

Letting Go of Your Cows: Release Your Old Habits and Ideas

Buddhist monk Thich Nhat Hanh tells of ancient stories in his 100+ published books. One of our favorites is the story of a wise man sitting with his disciples at the bend in a river. A distressed farmer approached them and asked, "Please can you help me? I can't find any of my cows. Have you seen them?" The wise man and his disciples shook their heads. They had not seen his cows.

The farmer anguished, "I'm so unhappy. I have twelve cows and I don't know why they all ran away. I have also a few acres of a sesame seed plantation and the insects have eaten up everything. I suffer so much I think I am going to kill myself."

The wise man said, "My friend, we have not seen any cows passing by here but you might look for them in the other direction."

The farmer thanked him and ran off. The wise man turned to his disciples and said, "You are the happiest people in the world. You don't have any cows to lose. If you have too many cows to take care of, you will be very busy."

The moral of the story is, "What do you own that you don't need?" Are you living in a house that's twice the size of what you need and too costly to maintain? Do the reasons why you originally bought the house still exist today? Similarly, do you own a stock in your portfolio that you inherited or purchased many years ago but wouldn't purchase today? Are the reasons you bought the stock years ago, the same reasons to keep the stock today?

Think of the things you have that prevent you from living your life in a new and different way because you own too many cows. Make sure the cows have a purpose.

Walter

Henry is a friend who exercises at my gym. Because Henry is a mortician, he possesses a thought-provoking perspective on life's purpose and meaning. One day while working out together, I asked him how he was feeling. He said, "Walter, health is wealth!"

"How so?" I replied.

Henry said, "People mistakenly believe the wealth they accumulate belongs to them and that they will live forever. They think that somehow they can take their wealth with them. With that, Henry started to laugh. He turned to me and said, "Walter, have you ever seen a hearse pulling a U-Haul trailer?"

Minor Decisions: Major Consequences

A loquacious pilot friend of mine owns a Cirrus GT airplane. He loves to talk about his flight travels. Occasionally, he takes me for a cruise into what he calls "the wild blue yonder" over the east end of Long Island. On a recent flight, I asked him about the navigation system. He said one of the most interesting aspects of flying the plane is that it takes just a slight movement of the joy stick to propel the plane way off course in only a few minutes.

Like his plane, seemingly inconsequential decisions we make about money can trigger major consequences down the road.

Allie

We had two young couples who began investing for retirement about the same time. During the first few months, the markets suffered a significant but temporary plunge. One couple recognized that this represented a buying opportunity and continued to save; the other couple panicked and decided to stop investing until the market recovered, against our advice. A year and a half later, the second couple still had not invested additional money into their account. The portfolio of the couple that continued to save had an annualized return of 3.5%, despite the initial downturn. The portfolio of the couple who stopped investing was up just 0.25%. The difference between the two accounts may not seem dramatic, but it's an example of how a small decision had a major impact on their investment returns.

This example also illustrates the importance of continuing to save and invest, even over a relatively short period of time. But if we extend the time period from 18 months to 18 or 20 years, the difference in the account balances becomes conspicuously greater.

Now let's assume those same two couples each started out saving $500 a month but one couple reduces their monthly contribution to $250 starting the third year. After just 20 years, the first couple has accumulated almost $100,000 more than the second couple.

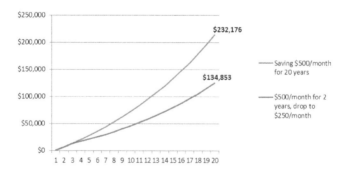

Above illustration assumes a 6% annualized return

Example is hypothetical and does not reflect actual savings in a client account and should be used for illustrative purposes only.

The blue line represents savings for $500/month, continuing for 20 years. Principle amount invested is $120,000. The red line represents savings of $500/month for two years, then dropping to a savings rate of $250/month for the remaining 18 years. Principle amount invested is $66,000.

Consider the major effect of the second couple's decision to make the apparently minor change of reducing their monthly savings by half. When flying an airplane, and especially when investing your money, avoid making small miscalculations that can cause your investment portfolio to suffer dramatically.

Your Next Best Ten Years

When discussing wealth management or financial planning, it is vital to include life goals that go beyond investments and stock market performance. The next best ten years beckon us to connect with what we really want from life. When we think about our best ten years, what decade are we thinking about? If we are 35 years old, are the best ten years of our life from 55-65? Our next best ten years are right now! What do we need to do **now** to have the most rewarding lifestyle?

The first choice is to consider our values. If actuarially we have 15, 20 or even 30 years to live and we have relatively good health and financial security, then the next best ten years should include the choices we wish to experience now. What is important to us about money, and what do we want it to do for us? Next, what would we like our top accomplishments to be, and what are our quality-of-life desires? Which relationships — spouse, children, siblings, parents, friends, etc. — are most important to us? What are some of our biggest worries that we need to overcome?

Training Your Mind

Walter

Quantum physics, the study of matter at the tiniest subatomic levels, is a fascinating field. I possess a cursory knowledge of the field, having read some works by scholars like Niels Bor, Albert Einstein and Max Planck. Their studies show that by merely observing subatomic particles under an electron microscope, you cause them to behave differently. In his book *Turning Point*, Fritjof Capra observes, "The crucial feature of quantum theory is that the observer is not only necessary to observe the properties of an atomic phenomenon, but is necessary to bring about these properties."

So, my conscious decision about how to observe an electron will determine the electron's properties to some extent. If I ask it a particle question, it will give a particle answer; if I ask it a wave question, it will give a wave answer. In other words, what is being observed changes, depending on who is doing the observing.

Capra continues, "The patterns scientists observe in nature are intimately connected with the patterns of their minds; with their concepts, thoughts and values. Thus, the scientific results they obtain and the technological applications they investigate will be conditioned by their frame of mind."

If this is true on the subatomic level, is it logical to assume it may be true at higher levels? If the consciousness of the observer can affect particles, then why can't we affect outcomes in our life based on how we choose to observe them? Suppose you intend to change careers and get an increase in salary. For a moment, imagine yourself as already having the new job. You are in that position and you've earned it. Your mind has no doubts that it will happen. You can feel the new job in your mind, your heart and your soul. You are connected with The Millionaire Within!

Finding your millionaire within is not just about money and accumulating wealth. It's also about finding a balance in your life that will allow doors to open and relationships to flourish. The millionaire within is already a part of you. It's been dormant. Wake it up! It might take twenty seconds or twenty years, depending on your ability to recognize this power.

If you can separate your money from fear, worry and emotion, you will be one step closer to unleashing **The Millionaire Within**.

"Whatever you can do or dream you can do, begin it.
Boldness has genius, power and magic in it!"
Frederick Goethe

Endnotes

[1] http://www.northstarfinancial.com/files/6314/6523/9571/2016_DALBAR_Advisor_Edition.pdf

[2] www.funderstanding.com

[3] U.S. Air Force Training Manual, chapter 1, lesson 5

[4] Daniel Kahneman and Mark W Riepe, "Aspects of Investor Psychology", Journal of Portfolio Management Vol 24, No 4 Summer 1998

[5] http://www.annualreviews.org/doi/full/10.1146/annurev-clinpsy-032813-153734

[6] Barry M Staw, "Knee-deep in the Big Muddy: A Study of Escalating Commitment to a Chosen Course of Action", Organizational Behavior and Human Performance Vol 16, Issue 1, June 1976

[7] Brad M Barber and Terrance Odean, "Boys Will be Boys: Gender, Overconfidence and Common Stock Investment," The Quarterly Journal of Economics Feb 2001

[8] Christine M. Riordan, "Three Ways Overconfidence Can Make a Fool of You," Forbes 8 Jan 2013

[9] Jay R Ritter, Behavioral Finance, Sept 2003

[10] Myles Udland, "Fidelity Reviewed Which Investors Did Best And What They Found Was Hilarious," Business Insider 4 Sept 2014.

[11] Jeff Stibel, "Why We Can't Predict Financial Markets," Harvard Business Review 22 Jan. 2009.

[12] James Montier, A Practitioner's Guide to Applying Behavioural Finance West Sussex, England, John Wiley & Sons Ltd, 2007

[13] Magda Kay, Psychology for Marketers 2012

[14] alternet.org

[15] psychcentral.com

[16] https://dqydj.com/stock-return-calculator-dividend-reinvestment-drip/

[17] "Mental Accounting," Shankar Vedantam, Washington Post May 19, 2007.

[18] Shengle Lin, "Stock Return and Financial Media Coverage Bias," University of California, Berkeley, 2011

[19] Hersh Shefrin, Santa Cara University, "How Psychological Pitfalls Generated the Global Financial Crisis," May 2009

[20] Dr. David Whitebread and Dr. Sue Bingham, "Habit Formation and Learning in Young Children," University of Cambridge 2008.

[21] Kate Levinson Ph D., Emotional Currency: A Woman's Guide to Building a Healthy Relationship with Money," (Berkeley CA: Celestial Arts, 2012).

[22] www.musicandmemory.org.

[23] Michael Morrison, "The Power of In-Store Music and its Influence on International Brands and Shopper Behavior: A Multi-Case Study Approach," April 2002.

[24] David Dobbs, "A Musician Who Performs With a Scalpel," New York Times 20 May 2008.

[25] Mihaly Csikszentmihalyi, Creativity: Flow and the Psychology of Discovery and Invention (New York, NY, H arper Perennial, 1996).

[26] Peter Economy, "Five Powerful Ways to Make Your Own Luck Every Day," Inc. 23 Jan 2015.

[27] "Be Happy: How to Make Your Own Luck," Women's Health 28 Mar 2014.

[28] David Winter, "Feeling Lucky: How Important is Luck to Career Success?" The Guardian 21 Feb 2011.

[29] Richard St. Johns, "Luck did not play a big part in Bill Gates' success," blog 10 Mar 2009.

[30] Aaron Zerah, How the Children Became Stars: A Family Treasury of Stories, Prayers and Blessings from Around the World Sorin Books, 2000

[31] Geoffrey James, Contributing Editor, "How to Create a Positive Attitude," Inc. 4 Feb 2013.

[32] Ben Geier, "What Did We Learn from the Dotcom Stock Bubble of 2000?" Time 12 Mar 2015.

[33] fundersandfounders.com

[34] Rick Ferri, "Any Monkey Can Beat The Market," Forbes 20 Dec 2012.

[35] Adam Backman, CFA, "Discover the Total Dividend Approach: Income and Growth from U.S. and International Dividend-Paying Stocks," Lord Abbett 7 Feb 2015.

[36] Morgan Housel, "How Almost Always Being Wrong Has Changed the Wall Street Analyst," The Motley Fool 27 Apr 2013.

[37] ibid

[38] Jeff Stibel, "Why We Can't Predict Financial Markets," Harvard Business Review 22 Jan 2009.

[39] financialfinesse.com

[40] Warren Buffet, "Why Stocks Beat Gold and Bonds," Fortune 9 Feb 2012.

[41] Caroline Fairchild, "Women CEOs in the Fortune 1000: By the numbers," Fortune 8 July 2014.

[42] Geraldine Sealey, "Women and Money," realsimple.com.

[43] changingstates.co.uk.

[44] "Divorce is Destroying Retirement," newsmax.com 17 Oct 2016.

[45] "The Changing Face of Retirement," Aegon, Transamerica Center for Retirement Studies 2014.

[6] https://learningenglish.voanews.com/a/a-23-2009-04-25-voa2-83141147/129694.html

[7] itwasneveradress.com

CPSIA information can be obtained
at www.ICGtesting.com
Printed in the USA
BVHW02*0213210418
513919BV00001B/1/P

9 781506 905112